MW00896097

NOTHING FOR TOMORROW

A Memoir

NANCY ROSSMAN

Copyright © 2014 Nancy Rossman
All rights reserved.

ISBN: 1500342033
ISBN 13: 9781500342036
Library of Congress Control Number: 2014911861
CreateSpace Independent Publishing Platform
North Charleston, South Carolina

For Lynda, the tallest woman I have ever known

PROLOGUE

LOOKING BACK, IT is fair to say Lynda became my best friend at a point in my life when I really needed one. We hurdled a fifteen-year age difference as well as my love affair with her twenty-year-old son when I was thirty-two.

"You're different, not what I expected," she said after our first meeting. I didn't agonize over what she meant or even suspect it was anything other than a compliment.

"You're exactly what I expected," I said. She laughed.

I met Lynda in 1978, six years after an emotionally charged exit from Ohio. My strong-willed, loving parents had been excellent role models during my childhood but left little room for departure from their beliefs as I became an adult with my own ideas. My decision to divorce my husband and give him primary custody of our infant daughter shamed my family. "If you leave Robin," my mother said, "I don't know if I'll ever love you again." Once I moved to Arizona in 1972, I found solace in a new job at Xerox, which gave me a sense of purpose. My success helped me overcome feelings of inadequacy and the money I earned gave me independence for the first time. I bought a small house in an older Tempe neighborhood, there was money to travel to Ohio to visit my daughter, and from an early age, she flew to Arizona during school holidays. The few times I revealed the story of Robin's custody to others, I saw shock on their faces. I became protective of how much I said about the arrangement, much less my reasons for making the decision I had made. I did not have a good friend, a person I trusted who would listen, offer advice, and soothe my bruised ego.

The first time I met Lynda, the feisty redhead, I laughed like my old self. I saw a brazen woman who spoke her mind and had an unusual sense of humor. There were no traces of damage or sadness in her life, that I could see. I wanted to be like her. Lynda seemed to be the kind of woman who would have lots of choices when it came to the people in her life. It was not evident to me that she also needed a friend. Also not evident to me was her suffering. I had no way of knowing she would need a confidant when she could no longer stand the pain that she had carefully hidden from everyone. As time went on and her pain threshold was pushed beyond tolerance, she gradually lost her enthusiasm for life, and she began to contemplate the possibility of opting out altogether. We argued and then not. My beliefs about the quality of life and who decides when enough is enough were strenuously tested. Even after she had made up her mind, she remained considerate of my feelings. Lynda finally said, "I'll wait until you understand."

Why did our bond come so easily? I only know that I never met a woman like her, not before or since, and that was over thirty years ago.

1

TIM

I T WAS AFTER five o'clock as I sat in my car and waited to turn left into Tempe's newly built Arizona Athletic Club. I rolled the windows down to take in the slight February breeze and smell the orange blossoms, two of my favorite things about spring time in Arizona. The sun glared into my eyes. When I pulled the visor down and glanced into the rearview mirror, a young blond guy in the sparkling clean BMW behind me smiled. His shaggy hair looked like planned disorder. I continued to stare. When the light changed the BMW sped past me.

He parked and was out of his car before I found a spot: tall, lean, completely outfitted in the white Fila tennis wear that Bjorn Borg had made popular. He looked in my direction. I turned around to see who had his attention, but there was no one behind me.

"I want to meet you," he said as he neared. "Tim Burns. I saw you last week but I was wrapped up in a tennis match." It sounded like a line, but I wasn't sure.

As he started to shake my hand he dropped his tennis racket. When he picked it up, he dropped his keys. We both laughed. At close range, his freckled face and dimpled cheeks reminded me of a grown-up Norman Rockwell kid: straight teeth, chocolate eyes, a sincere air about him.

"So, what're you here for?" he said. We ambled up the sidewalk between the Olympic-sized swimming pool and the tennis courts. Orange and red lantana made colorful ground cover, softening all the hardscape. Strategically placed palm trees gave the outside of the club pizzazz.

"I do some of everything—aerobics, running, weights, and anything that will keep me in shape," I said.

Tim opened the front door of the club for me. Liz, the sexy brunette at the reception desk, came alive when we walked in. Usually all I saw from her was attitude. She leaned over the sign-in sheet.

"Tim, hey," she said and dropped her eyes. "I haven't seen you lately." He ignored her. She continued to hold onto the pen.

He took it out of her hand without making eye contact and signed his name with a barely legible scribble. All I could make out was the T. He turned to me, "So, can I buy you a salad in a couple of hours?"

Liz reeled back, losing her balance and almost falling off the stool. Tim's offer shocked me even more.

"Sure," I said. Maybe he was just being friendly

He tapped my back with his tennis racket and winked. "See you in the bar around seven."

I struggled through the aerobics class distracted by thoughts of Tim. I couldn't remember my last date, but it had been two years since I attempted having a boyfriend. Things hadn't worked out for me in the dating scene. It probably was my fault: I wouldn't let anyone close; I didn't feel worthy of attention. The few times I'd introduced my dates to Robin, she always found something wrong with them. "You aren't exactly approachable," my work friends told me.

An extra long shower and cold plunge didn't calm me. I fretted about my outfit, even though khaki shorts and a gauze blouse was an upgrade from my usual getup after a workout. I blow-dried my shoulder-length brown hair as straight as I could after the humidity from the shower. My hand shook as I put on a light pink lipstick and blush. I took one last look in the mirror and turned my head side to side. My hazel eyes and turned-up nose were still my best assets.

When I left the women's locker room, I passed the racket ball and handball courts, all occupied. I shook my head—it looked so dangerous. I remembered how, when we were kids, my brother had teased me that I'd never learn to play softball if I was afraid to catch the ball.

My throat dried up as I passed the gymnasium and climbed the stairs to the club bar. Most of the tables in the café were full. People laughed and talked over the music and the sound of a college basketball game playing on the TV over the bar. It took several seconds before I saw Tim at a table on the outdoor patio overlooking the tennis courts. He stood as I approached and pulled out a chair. An ice bucket, a bottle of wine, and two glasses sat on the corner of the table.

"There's a hot game in progress," he said and pointed at the courts. "The young guy is on the tennis team with me at ASU."

I peeked over Tim's shoulder down onto the court and grinned. The other guy was my age. "Bet the old guy wins," I said.

Tim and I sipped wine and played getting-to-know-you. He had two older brothers, whereas I had a younger brother and sister. My father died when I was twenty, and his died when he was ten. He stuttered through the explanation.

"It was a plane crash. A small plane. Everyone died," he said and rubbed his temple for several seconds. I gave him time.

"That's awful," I said.

"Devastating for me, but Lynda was only thirty-nine," he said. He must have noticed my puzzled stare.

"Lynda, my mother."

"You call her Lynda?" I asked.

He sat back in his chair. "Once, as a smart-ass teenager, I called her that when she bugged me about something. I thought she'd swear at me, but she grinned and said she rather liked it. It stuck."

"Fascinating," I finally said. *Weird.*

He glanced back at the court. "What's your story?"

"Where to start, what to leave out is always the dilemma," I said. He waved his hand. "Tell me all of it."

"No chapter and verse. Short version. Grew up on an Ohio farm, married my college sweetheart as soon as I graduated, taught school for five years, had a baby, divorced, moved to Arizona six years ago in 1972, and have been selling for Xerox ever since."

I wrung my hands and sat back. He nodded for me to continue.

"When my ex-husband and I divorced I decided, finally, that my daughter would be better off with her father. Sam had wanted to have a baby so badly and from the start it was he who nurtured her and devoted himself to her. My family practically disowned me," I continued. "It kept me in a black hole for years."

Tim leaned forward, never taking his eyes off me. "How old is your daughter now?"

"Robin is eight." I couldn't keep eye contact. It stunned me that I had just revealed the most private thing in my life. Tears were close.

Talking about leaving Robin in Sam's care still wrenched my gut. My mother and siblings continued to look at me sideways even though everyone praised Sam's parenting—his skill made it worse for me. It was hard to admit that between the two of us, he was more patient, more curious about a child's thought, more open, more affectionate, and less selfish.

Tim moved his chair in closer. "But you see her?" I nodded. "Is she as cute as you?"

I smiled as every tense muscle in my neck slacked. I pictured her with arms akimbo, curly blond hair, turned up nose and hazel eyes—very much like mine—teasing me about something stupid I'd done.

Another hour passed. Maybe Tim's energy intoxicated me, or maybe it was his youth. He talked about tennis and working out; restaurants around town; college life and how he'd finally settled on a business major. There wasn't much common ground, but I felt relaxed. By the time we decided to leave, the parking lot had nearly emptied. He walked with me to my car, took the keys from my hand and unlocked the door.

"How about Friday night we do this again?" he asked as he knelt outside the car to be at eye level with me.

That is such a bad idea. That is such a great idea.

I fumbled for the seat belt.

"C'mon. Don't worry about it. We're adults," he said.

"I'm more adult than you," I pointed out.

He shrugged. "If you give me your card, I'll call you at your office tomorrow with a plan, okay?" I had hardly handed one over before he turned and left.

I drove the four miles to my house in a daze. The road stretched ahead like a tangled ribbon, dotted on both sides by mature trees. Each street had its own personality, but still, at night all the turnoffs looked the same. Without thinking, I turned south on Priest Drive instead of Carter Drive where I lived. *I am such a fool.*

Mabel Murphy's, the "in" disco just off the ASU campus, did not heed the maximum occupancy code. Sweaty bodies competed with sweet perfumes as we threaded our way through the crowd. Along the way, Tim introduced me to waitresses, an occasional patron, and the disc jockey. Finally we slipped into a reserved booth. Changing colored lights illuminated the rotating mirrored balls. Multiple speakers splashed music across the two-level dance floor.

Tim had called me several days before to lay out our Friday plans. In the hours before he came to pick me up, I'd frantically scoured my closet for something cool to wear. Not the tube top, not jeans, not the strapless sundress with the lace-up bodice but the maroon Danskin body suit and matching skirt. The crisscross front showed more cleavage than I remembered from when I had tried it on in the store. Last came the strapped high heels and a check in the full-length mirror. I'd twirled and watched the skirt flare out to reveal the leotard underneath—then obsessed about whether it was too much until Tim arrived, dressed for seduction in white pants, a starched blue checked shirt, and a navy blazer. My thoughts of too much had wilted to under-dressed, but he whistled.

"You look gorgeous," he'd said.

Now, Tim rubbed my arm. "Stayin' Alive" filled the room. "How about it?" he said as he stood and led the way.

John Travolta had nothing on Tim, who moved to the rhythm with his whole body. His steps were fluid and dramatic, but easy to follow. We stayed on the dance floor for three more songs. He knew when to stop and patiently teach me a maneuver. "Watch me and then I'll do it with you. Try it again."

Finally, I needed a breather. I was headed back to our booth when "How Deep Is Your Love" began playing. The lights dimmed. Tim caught my hand and twirled me into his arms.

"I don't want to wait another minute to hold you," he whispered in my ear. His hand moved down into the small of my back.

Several hours later, we drove the few miles to my house in silence. Normally Mill Avenue was thick with cars, but not then. It took everything to stay calm and not blurt out thank you, thank you. I needed all of it.

"I had a good time, Nancy," he said. I glimpsed at him but wanted to stare and replay the whole night in my mind.

He parked the car and walked me toward the front door but stopped short. He rested his right hand on my neck. Slowly, he pulled me closer. The kiss was luscious. Passionate, but so light it left me wanting.

"Penny for your thoughts," he said and backed away.

For a million I might tell you. Might.

"I had fun."

He gave me a thumbs-up and headed back to the car. "I'll run with you in the morning if you want."

"On Saturday I go at six. You sure you're up for it?"

He groaned. "See you then."

I stood at the door and watched his tail lights disappear. I crossed my arms over my chest and rocked back and forth, humming, "Sweet Wonderful You." I felt dizzy, like a girl with a hula hoop. Five minutes passed before I padded into the house and back to my bedroom. In low light the mirror was kind. I removed all my clothes and stared at my image. I turned and looked back over my shoulder. *Hmm.*

The next morning Tim showed up promptly at six. We wasted no time in starting our four-mile run.

"You pace us," he said. I set my watch for a ten-minute mile.

He breathed easily. "Running isn't a regular thing but at this pace, I could go all day," he jabbed me and leaped out in front.

I caught him and we ran fifteen minutes without talking. Then I picked it up. The jog became a run.

He stared straight ahead, his breath labored. "How far have we gone?"

I pointed to a green shed at the far end of the city park we had entered. "See that building up ahead, on the left?" His eyes followed my finger. We stayed on the sidewalk as it twisted and turned through the flat park.

"That's halfway. You okay?" I said. He nodded and sighed.

In no time we had circled the green shed and were on the return path home. We increased our speed again, like horses heading for the barn. Neither of us relented. We raced out of the park across Baseline Road. As with all runners who hit the bricks daily, my body knew just how much energy to expend. When we reached the school crossing sign, I knew only four-tenths of a mile remained. Competition took over. My breathing went from heavy to gasping. Tim dropped back.

Back at the house, I sprawled out on the damp grass and rolled over on my back. After a minute or so Tim limped up the driveway.

"What was that?" he chided. "Not one bit of fun." He collapsed beside me.

Eventually we rose and strolled into the house. In the living room, we sat across from one another on brown corduroy love seats. He relaxed back into the cushions like he was prepared to stay awhile. His stare unnerved me. I rubbed my leg even though it didn't ache. Then I moved to the bookcase and searched through my limited tape selection.

"I know what you need," he said. I gave him my best nonchalant shrug.

"A cat," he said. "Don't all single women have a cat?"

"I'm not that much of a pet person," I said. "Too many years growing up on a farm with animals everywhere." I put on Neil Diamond.

"That's right, the farmer's daughter," he said. "Can't say I ever met one."

"What about you, any pets?" I said. *Keep talking. Stay. Let me look for flaws.*

— 7 —

He grinned. "My first was a rabbit named Harold. Lynda got him for me one Easter—she thought it would be fun because all the other kids had dogs and cats. She had no idea the rabbit would grow up to be so big and so mean. How traumatic, to be afraid of my Easter bunny. We still laugh about it."

"Lynda sounds like a hip mother," I said. "Mine's a bit conventional and judgmental."

When I walked him out to his car, we stood there long enough for it to be uncomfortable. He shuffled his feet. Everything was unexplored territory.

I need a shower, breakfast, and sex. Wonder if he eats breakfast.

He climbed into the car. "I'll call you."

The first three days of the week ticked by without a word from Tim. Each night I rushed to the Athletic Club hoping to see him. Accidentally, of course, each time I checked in, Liz gave me the once-over times ten. I once almost asked her if she'd seen Tim but instantly congratulated myself for restraint. As I walked away, I laughed out loud about the situation I was in: a crush on cute guy who hadn't yet had his twenty-first birthday. Ridiculous, yet more tempting than a box of chocolate to a dieter.

Finally, on Thursday, he called me, and after that we began to see each other regularly. Three weeks went by faster than I could have imagined. There were weekend dates, occasional meet-ups after a club workout. Everything felt natural, except that Tim still had not made a real move on me. It confused me. I mentally replayed the dates on my way to work while cars zipped by me on I-10. I imagined phoning in to Crazy Dave at KUPD with my dilemma and giggled. He'd have a field day with my question: How do I seduce a twenty-year-old?

One morning I pulled into the parking garage off Central Avenue and found my reserved space. "Business is easier than life," I thought. Still immersed in my own world, it took me a moment to notice that Joe had driven into his space at the same time.

A few weeks earlier Joe and I had been made business partners, as an experiment. I liked him. His sales skills outshone most, he was handsome without the ego, and he had been a star running back at Notre Dame. He'd even had a short pro career until he blew out his knee. You'd have thought he still played the game, the way men gushed over him when he introduced himself. I got a kick out of the drama, but it embarrassed Joe. His reaction made him more human. An understated idol.

We made small talk about the weather and traffic as we walked into the office. At our desks, we picked up our day timers and files, and headed for a conference room to plan our week. Within thirty minutes, we'd set our goals, identified who would make which calls and give which demonstrations, and figured out what proposals needed to be written.

"So, Nancy, where have you been lately?" he asked as we headed back to the bullpen. "Haven't seen you after work at Durant's in a while."

For a second I thought he was baiting me. "I met someone and, well, it has consumed me."

He frowned. "Who is he? Maybe I know him."

Several salesmen sat at their desks, either on the phone or doing paperwork. The six-hundred-square-foot windowless bullpen housed ten of us with all of the privacy of a gang shower. Our sales manager liked to say that he didn't want us to be comfortable in the office. "Nothing gets sold here," he would complain, heading for his plush office and then shutting the door behind him.

"Trust me, Joe. You don't know him," I said.

A couple of guys looked up when they realized what we were talking about. Over the years I learned that men want to hear the gossip as much as women.

"He doesn't work for the competition, does he?" Joe asked.

I shook my head. "He's at ASU."

"Wow. A professor doesn't sound like your type," he said. Someone blurted out agreement.

"Not a professor you doofus, a student," I said without contemplating how it would sound.

Joe laughed hard and plopped down in his desk chair. He kept it up until he noticed my stone face. I picked up my phone and dialed my own house, pretending to talk with a customer. Out of the corner of my eye, I saw Joe watching me. He pulled out his bottom desk drawer and propped up a leg. He stared a little longer and then smiled like he suddenly remembered something very pleasant, a distant memory.

After I hung up, he leaned toward me. "You'd each be in your sexual prime. No doubt, you've thought of that."

The room quieted instantly. Low mumbles and chuckles eventually followed. "*What* about sex? *What* about Nancy?" They talked over each other.

"It's not that I'm trying to keep it a secret," I said. "I'm just not granting interviews."

Finally, one Wednesday night Tim called and asked to come over. He arrived at six with a chilled bottle of champagne. It confused and delighted me.

"What are we celebrating?" I asked.

He headed for the kitchen and uncorked the Dom Perignon, then poured for each of us.

"To you," he said and clinked glasses. We sipped.

He downed the rest of his champagne. In one swoop he wrapped his arms around me. His lips moved across my cheek to my neck, each kiss longer than the one before. Finally, very slowly he backed me down the hallway to the bedroom. Somewhere I kicked off my high heels as he undid my skirt and let it fall to the floor. Both of us were naked by the time we reached the bed, where he laid me down and stretched himself beside me.

Maybe twenty minutes passed or maybe it was an hour. I couldn't believe how much he knew—all the important parts, the affection, the passion, and his endurance.

Afterward, he stroked my hair. "That takes some pressure off the end of the night," he said. "Maybe just a quick nap and then we'll head out." He fell asleep in seconds. I stared for some time and relived the memory of unbridled lust. His contented sleep made me jealous.

Now what? passed through my mind. I chastised myself, I congratulated myself, and then finally, I laid my head on the pillow.

When I woke up, it took several seconds before my eyes focused on the neon dial. Ten o'clock. Tim stirred.

"Hey," he muttered. "Know what? I'm starved."

A burger never tasted better. I thought it was all the activity, and the lateness of the hour, but then I realized it was the only meal I'd had all day. I dipped a French fry in ketchup. The Chuckbox restaurant overflowed with college students in various combinations of denim and tee shirts. *Am I the oldest person here?*

I watched Tim eat. He stopped every now and then, wiping away stray mustard. Snippets of our lovemaking popped into my mind.

"How did you learn so much about women?" I blurted out.

He put his burger down. "I'm not sure how to answer that."

"Have you had lots of girlfriends?" I said, going right to the real question that plagued me.

He squinted upward, like the answer was written on the ceiling. "I lost my virginity when I was fourteen. Karen. She was Lynda's good friend. Well, until that happened."

The tone of his answer was so unaffected he could have been giving me the weather report. I sat back, suddenly not hungry. "How in the world did that happen?" I said. "I mean, if you don't mind."

Tim looked up at the ceiling again. "Karen's husband split with his secretary. Didn't leave a note or anything. A week later he called and said he wouldn't be back. She was devastated. After that, she spent a lot of time at our house. One day she dropped by while Lynda was out. I don't think she planned it, but she might have. She suggested we go for a swim and, well, the rest is history."

"So it was that one time?" I said. He nodded.

"It was forever, forever, ago. She taught me a lot. And no matter what Lynda thought, she was a nice person. I felt sorry for her," he said as he eyed my plate. "Aren't you going to finish yours?"

I pushed my half-eaten burger his way, still wondering just how much experience he'd had and how the experience with Karen had affected him. *Change the subject. Change the subject.*

"Tell me about Lynda," I said.

"She's attractive. Some say she looks like Jill St. John and I'll tell you, she loves that," he said. "And even though she's not an artist, she has an artistic personality—and eccentric. You'll see what I mean."

We rode home with the windows down enjoying the balmy March night. Neil Diamond's "Longfellow Serenade" played in the background. Tim knew it was one of my favorites, as opposed to something he'd pick, like Prince.

After he dropped me off, I paced so much I expected to see the carpet thread bare where I'd walked from the living room to the dining room and back. I did a load of wash, reorganized my closet, and ironed. Ironed! By 2 a.m. I was exhausted. Sleep came quickly, followed by a dream.

I stood in front of an enormous Gothic church. When I started to walk up the front steps, they went on forever, as if I were climbing the wrong way on an escalator. The train on my frilly wedding dress caught on everything. Finally, I got to the top as the church doors opened. Hundreds of people stood and smiled as I strolled down the aisle. Joyful organ music played and white rose petals littered my path. I neared the altar where a minister stood. Out of nowhere a groom, the size of a ring bearer, appeared and peeked up at me. He smiled to reveal baby teeth.

The next morning I got to work late. Joe stood at the reception desk as I picked up my messages. He sprinted to catch up with me as I headed back to the bullpen. "What's the occasion?" he asked. I frowned.

"You weren't out on calls?" he said. I shook my head.

We rounded the corner. To my embarrassment, an enormous vase with red roses sat on my desk, two dozen at least. I sat down, smelled them, and turned the vase all the way around before I saw the card. My hand shook as I opened it.

N—you're more than a woman. Love, Tim

I sighed and put the card in my lap, then, reread it. I felt the guys' eyes on me, but I didn't look up before diving into the day's work.

"When do I get to meet your outrageous mother?" I asked Tim two days later. He looked stunned but quickly recovered. "How about Sunday?"

Any other time, meeting a guy's mother had always taken a lot longer and meant something serious. I didn't consider that now, Tim's relationship with Lynda intrigued me. In a way, I envied him.

Lynda's driveway was hedged by manicured shrubs and clustered flowerpots overflowing with a riot of color. Through wrought-iron gates we entered a lush courtyard where an exquisite tiled pool stretched along the front of the house and disappeared around the corner. The house's single-story Spanish architecture was enhanced by a double mud-tiled roof, antique black lights, and hardware. Giant pink oleander lined the entire front wall of the house, creating a soft backdrop. Hibiscus and jasmine complemented each other in color and size.

"Wow," I said.

Tim rang the bell while I smoothed my sundress. First-time anything always unnerved me. My mouth was dry as dirt.

The late afternoon sunshine and slight breeze tingled on my skin. From somewhere inside the house I heard music. Tim rang the bell again. Finally, he pulled keys from his pocket and led me into the foyer. As we entered he called out, "Ma, we're here."

We waited, looked around and he continued. "Hey, Lynda ... where the hell are you?"

He motioned for me to sit as he wandered down the hall. I perched on the edge of a plush, off-white sectional and surveyed the room. Multiple shades of white and tan with occasional black accents showcased slate floors. Thick tribal rugs pulled it all together. Elegant, comfortable, and understated. A single piece of artwork hung over the sectional. It was massive, and the bold brush strokes had heavy ridges, but the overall effect was soft because of the colors. I stared at it long enough to decide it was a painting of a horse, although I wouldn't have bet money on it.

"I don't know where she is," said Tim as he rejoined me. "Her car is gone, so she's probably on a quick errand. I'm usually late."

Just then, a door opened down the hall, followed by commotion and clatter. A black cocker spaniel bounded into the living room. Lynda's laughter and expletives filled the room with energy before she appeared. She entered holding a grocery bag and stopped abruptly. She smiled. "Oh my god," she said to Tim, "You look exactly like my son. But you can't be. You're on time."

She set down the grocery bag and took my hand in both of hers. "Nancy, I'm delighted to meet you. You're even prettier than Tim said. Let's go into my new gourmet kitchen where no one cooks but there's atmosphere and good wine."

Tim and I lagged behind her. With her red hair and fabulous petite figure, she could easily have been mistaken for Jill St. John. Her huge brown eyes and Colgate smile took me in. Later, I would realize that Lynda's sarcasm and self-effacing humor reminded me of Joan Rivers. Tim kept the wine glasses full while Lynda kept me riveted.

"Isn't this kitchen something?" she said as she spread her arms out. "Tall cabinets, tiled backsplash, butcher block. Almost inspires me. But then, hell—I just make a reservation. Don't want to get anything dirty."

"That was the idea, Lynda. When we took the cooking classes in L.A.," Tim said. I turned to Lynda, who sat next to me.

"Okay, so I had some fun with the chef. He knew more about cooking in the bedroom than in the kitchen. But at least you learned how to cook, Timothy."

When the laughter died down I asked Lynda if she had a boyfriend. "No, god no," she said. "Some time after Peter died, I started dating. I've already had the good and the bad. With my luck, the next would be boring."

"Ma, ease up will you?" Tim said. "Nancy's meeting you for the first time."

Lynda waved him off. "I have an occasional crush, mind you," she said. "Those are fun, and always short-lived."

The dog took up residence next to my chair. I reached down to pet him just to be polite.

"Ralph is his name," Lynda said. "He's a little neurotic."

"Like his owner," Tim whispered.

Lynda scowled and threw a wine cork at him. "Hey, are we eating soon? I don't want to get snockered in front of your lovely girlfriend."

Girlfriend.

We pulled into Avanti's parking lot. The posh restaurant lobby was jammed with anxious patrons dressed in their finest. A hostess approached with a waiting list. Tim stepped forward with bills in his fist. "We had a reservation, party of three," he said.

"Smooth," Lynda said to me. "How much did he give her?" I shrugged.

Tim ordered wine while we studied the extensive menu. Lynda licked her lips as she muttered, "Oh boy, I love prime rib but I know I should have fish. Damn. I walked Ralph three times today to get exercise in case I caved. I want something big but light. Do you think they do that in beef?"

I giggled. The waiter approached to tell us about the specials. He made eye contact with each of us as he enthusiastically rolled through his list. "Tonight we have broiled New Zealand lamb chops with a mint glaze, baked apples, and vegetable medley. Next—"

Lynda interrupted, "Young man, what's in your medley?"

The waiter scratched his head. "Actually, I remember green beans and zucchini, but I don't know what else."

"If they call it a 'medley,' can they charge more than if they called it mixed vegetables?" she said.

He nodded and gave a slight laugh. "Maybe."

"You bet your bippy they can," she said as she lifted her wine glass. "Listen, forget the rest, just tell me about the prime rib. Can I have a grand cut, from the end? I'm a good tipper. I have references."

Tim smirked at me. After the waiter left, Lynda looked back and forth between us with a devilish grin on her face. "What?" she said.

Lynda was curious about my Ohio farm upbringing. Most of all she wanted to hear about the animals. What kind? How many? She leaned in as I described the cows and horses. She seemed to be picturing it and wishing it had been her experience. She looked deflated when I finally confessed that I hated the whole scene.

"But you must have loved all the quiet, open space, the simple life?" she said.

I shook my head. "That's exactly what I disliked the most. All those frogs croaking in the still night air, so many they echoed. I told Dad we should shoot one as an example to the rest."

"You bad girl," she laughed. "Did your father know how much you disliked the farm? It must have hurt his feelings."

"No, not at all. From the time I was ten years old I told everyone I wanted to marry a boy from Cleveland and move to the city. Meaning, I considered Cleveland the pinnacle of places to live."

Tim and Lynda roared. When the laughter died down, she scowled and glanced off in the distance as if she were solving an algebra problem.

"Why is Cleveland the butt of so many jokes?" she wondered. "Comedians use it in their routines and you hear it in the movies. Is it that bad?"

"Well, some weird things have happened there," I told her. "During a massive urban renewal project the Cuyahoga River caught on fire—due to all the oil and other flammable pollutants. They couldn't extinguish it, they had to let it burn itself out."

After our waiter interrupted my history lesson with our first course, I turned to Tim. "Tell me about your brothers. I only know that you're the youngest."

Several seconds passed. Tim gave Lynda a sidelong glance.

She moved forward and cleared her throat. "Nancy, I married David and had two sons. But David played around on me and he was a pain in the ass. I divorced him and married his younger brother, Peter. The love of my life." She bent her head down before she continued. "And that is why I say that Timothy is my love child."

She sat back in her seat, rigid and expressionless. She picked up her wine glass and waited for my reaction.

"We have something in common, Lynda," I said. She raised an eyebrow. "I've also been married. And you know what? You don't have an exclusive on bad choices."

Lynda's shoulders relaxed as she reached out and patted my hand. "Well said, cookie. Did you learn your lesson?"

Right from the start, Lynda was comfortable to be with. I loved to laugh, and she liked an audience. The more I chuckled, the funnier she became. Tim said I encouraged her. She made fun of herself first and foremost, but she didn't spare her sons and other family members, either. My father had been similar in that way, so I felt at home.

"Tell me about your brothers," I asked Tim again one morning, "and cousins."

He nodded. "We look alike for starters. There's John, the serious accountant type, and Todd, the terrorist."

Tim and I were drinking coffee and sharing the newspaper. We had been debating his offer to do some yard work for me while I read over his English term paper on the growing popularity of female authors. Somehow I'd convinced him that I knew something about the subject, when all I wanted was an excuse to see him. Some reason to make him appear an extra time. It was a lazy day—I was luxuriating in doing nothing for a bit, enjoying the moment. His classes, seeing Lynda, seeing me, exercise, and tennis filled Tim's days, while I had work and worry on my plate.

"My brothers ... we're so different," he sighed and glanced out the window. "But you don't get to pick your family. And then there's Lynda. She excuses her shortcomings by saying motherhood wasn't on her A-list. John doesn't seem to care one way or another about people, and Todd is a pressure cooker waiting to blow. Everything makes him angry."

I poured more coffee. "So you're the child closest to Lynda."

"Peter was the love of her life, as she said. Maybe the only positive thing that happened to her. I look like him; she says I am like him," he said and twisted the gold ring he always wore.

It had an antique look about it. Some sort of emblem. Tim noticed how it caught my eye.

"It was his college ring. Princeton," he said. His eyes filled momentarily. We sat in silence for several minutes.

After Tim gathered up the tools from the shed and disappeared into the back-yard, I picked up his term paper and tried to read. It didn't have my attention. I grabbed the phone and dialed Robin.

She answered on the first ring in her most grown-up voice, "Berry residence."

I pictured her dressed in a Girl Scout uniform, ready for her Saturday troop meeting. Her voice was sunshine.

"How's school, honey?" I stood up and wiped off the kitchen counter.

"It's good. I'll get all A's again, I think. But Mom ... I have a secret to tell you," she whispered.

"Okay," I said.

"Daddy has a girlfriend."

I sat down. "Really?"

"Yeah, she's an actress," she said.

That made me grin. An actress? In Ohio? Robin must have messed up the facts, but I didn't want to push it.

"He met her at church—right after she found the lord. Well, that's what Dad said, anyway."

"Do you like her?" I asked.

"I dunno," she said. I imagined her trademark shoulder shrug, which usually accompanied dunno. "I haven't met her yet."

"How come?" I said.

"Dad says he'll see how it goes. He said he's not sure she's serious enough for him."

"Serious about what?" I said.

"The lord."

I struggled to bury the laughter I felt brewing, but her well-honed radar made it tough for me to conceal.

"Are you laughing at me again?" she said.

"No, just smiling. We'll be together in a month, remember? Easter vacation. Swimming in the big pool at the club, playing with Tracy next door. Anything special you want to do?"

After we said our goodbyes, I sat back down. Sam had a girlfriend. It pleased me. Plenty of time had passed, enough for both of us to move on. Six years had mended many fences. I wondered what Robin would make of Tim.

I shook my head in disbelief as I continued to sit at the kitchen table. If I hadn't been so naïve, I wouldn't have married Sam in the first place. He was the kind of guy I'd always pictured myself marrying: from a good family, nice looking, athletic. I'd been a twenty-one-year-old virgin, full of Cinderella fantasies about marriage. After our wedding, it became clear that Sam wanted to make all the decisions, just like his father had done. He controlled the money, and he wanted me to stay at home and have children. I tried to reason with him, but my arguments fell flat. His motto was, "A ship can only have one master."

The first year I was in Arizona my mother and I had no contact. The trouble between us stemmed from the day I left Ohio, when she issued her ultimatum. I couldn't believe that she wouldn't love me.

My hands had trembled as I gripped the steering wheel and drove off. Not a word. Not a glance in the rearview mirror. But plenty of tears, tremendous exhaustion, and my most fervent prayer: *Please let me be right*.

After a month or so, Mom sent me a letter. I returned it, unopened. She mailed a birthday gift and later a Christmas gift, both of which I returned. She phoned and I didn't answer. Until one day, when over a year had passed, she phoned and I picked up.

"Please Nancy. Don't cut me out of your life. I was wrong. I am so sorry," Mom said. She choked the words out between sobs.

I broke down. She was my mother. Maybe she was beginning to understand.

The phone rang and pulled me out of a memory that felt like it happened yesterday instead of years earlier.

"Nancy dear," Mom said. "What are you up to this morning?"

Almost as if my thoughts had made it happen. And it wasn't the first time. *Hope I'm not a witch.*

"Just getting ready to wash clothes and change the sheets," I told her. "Some jobs are the same whether you're married or single."

She laughed. We chatted briefly, and it felt good to hear her voice—the lilt of her Southern drawl. It had been over thirty years since she'd lived in Georgia, but she still had the accent. It had to take work to keep it.

Maybe things could go back to the way they were. I wanted to talk to her about Tim and Lynda, but I chickened out. I decided that the next time we talked, I'd broach the subject.

NANCY ROSSMAN

I padded down the hall toward the laundry room. A few minutes later I felt a thump on the shoulder that spooked me.

"Hey," Tim said. "You're a million miles away. What's going on?"

I pulled towels from the dryer. "Thinking about the phone calls with my daughter and mother. Both left me feeling a little blue."

He grabbed my hand. "Lynda wants to barbeque at her house tomorrow. Maybe around four?" I smiled and twirled a long tress of hair around my finger.

She was so funny. Wish I could be as confident as she is. Wonder what she really thinks about all this.

Lynda's music blared throughout the house. Some instrumental jazz stuff. The only kind of music I never bought. She hummed as she fixed white sangrias for us and a scotch for Tim.

Scotch. Isn't that what dads drink?

"The worst thing about being fifty is getting my AARP card in the mail," she said. She forced a laugh but I knew she meant it.

"I think there are worse things," I said.

She handed me a chilled oversized wine glass filled to the brim over crushed ice with an orange wedge and a cherry. I sampled and smacked my lips. "Delicious." It was nearly ninety degrees and only March, so this was just what I needed.

She sat beside me and then decided we should move out to the covered patio and enjoy the pool. The L-shaped- pool was visible from both the kitchen and living room before it disappeared around the side of the house to the bedroom wing. The end near us had a swim-up bar like you'd see in a Conde Nast magazine. Very showy. If you weren't in the pool, you could take a few stairs down into a tiled pit that held a fridge and sink.

Lynda's cocker spaniel, Ralph, joined us. He had been raised by her and knew his place, his neurosis mostly in check. He rested his head under her hand for a stroke. "If only men were as respectful and patient," she said.

We sat on deck chairs and sipped our sangrias while Tim talked on the phone inside. I stretched my legs out and yawned.

"So, if you hate getting your AARP card, how will you feel about being called grandma?" I teased.

She shook her head. "I swear if everyone knew how quickly children become teenagers—and it just never stops—they'd have more dogs."

"But you had three children," I said.

She moved out of her chair to sit beside Ralph on the floor. He nuzzled up against her, his tail wagging the whole time. She scratched his ears and under his chin.

"Women didn't think about having children in my day. They just did it. After my second child I thought I'd need to have myself committed but instead, I had a third. Tim. There's nothing sane about a decision to have children. But enough about me," she said. "What's your opinion?"

I squirmed. "I'd say I didn't want to but got talked into it. Sam, my college sweetheart and husband, begged for a child. We debated for months. There was more support for his wish, from our families."

The drink didn't taste good anymore. I set it down on the small table next to my chair, then crossed my legs and rested my chin in my hand. She watched me. When I finally looked up, she motioned for me to continue with a gentle wave of her hand.

"The decision to end the five-year marriage was easy. He wanted a wife like his mother: a woman who did volunteer work, not one who wanted a career. He told me once that *Taming of the Shrew* reminded him of his marriage to me. It stunned me but he thought it was funny. He also thought that if a woman wanted sex more than her husband, she must be a nymphomaniac. He even sent me to the doctor for an examination, because he suspected I had that problem."

Lynda sighed and brushed dog hair off her shorts. She picked up my drink and handed it back to me. It was a good idea. Cold and tangy.

"So, ending the marriage was easy. Contrary to that, we talked tirelessly about who should have primary custody of Robin. He was in the best position both financially and geographically since he wanted to remain in Ohio surrounded by family and life-long friends. I relented. It was, and perhaps still is, an embarrassment and disappointment for my family. Especially my mother, although we've been speaking more lately."

Lynda cleared her throat. "Do you see Robin?"

I nodded. "She flies out at Easter, and for two weeks in the summer, and then again in the fall. All by herself, since she was five. She's eight now."

"Hey honey, not to worry. If things are improving be happy. It sounds like you were number one on the hit parade and then crashed. Think of it as a car wreck. You can fix it. Just takes time. Not like my mother, Marie, who never liked me. Marie makes Joan Crawford look like Doris Day."

I giggled and had another sip. "Are you sure you're not exaggerating just to make me feel better?"

She couldn't hide a mischievous grin. Finally, she winked. "Where the heck is Timothy?"

2

LADIES' TENNIS

OTHER THAN TAKING care of Ralph, Lynda's favorite activity was tennis. Not just playing the game, but practicing, shopping for outfits, and watching professional matches. The sport consumed at least two hours of her daily schedule. Tim had often practiced his game with her, but it put a crimp in their relationship. Plus, she preferred the deference the club pro showed her. She bragged about the cost to Tim, who always said that whatever the guy charged her, it wasn't enough. Then they'd laugh.

"I'd like to get back into tennis," I said one day. It stopped Lynda and Tim; neither said a word. "What?" I said. "I used to play. Worked my way up to the C's."

They bent over with laughter. It got worse when I explained that it took me almost two years to get to the C level and by then, I'd lost my enthusiasm for the game. Ladies' tennis leagues were brutal, worse than business.

Lynda smiled broadly. "I'd love to get you back on the court. I need a practice partner. In exchange, I could help you shop for clothes and equipment. What do you say?"

Tim shook his head and left the room.

"He thinks it's a bad idea?" I asked.

"Who cares?" she shrugged. "He's probably worried about my competitive streak—there have been episodes. But I now believe that the game takes a back seat to the company and exercise. My prior focus was the win, but now I go for good form in a great outfit ... followed by a gourmet lunch."

Lynda grabbed her calendar to make a date to get started. She seemed excited about the whole idea and I wanted to know more about her.

"So tell me about the ladies at your club," I said. She stood up like she was taking center stage. "Now, about the ladies—some of the bitches play down a flight so that they can always win. Then there are others who I swear can't see the line and call fair balls out. No doubt this is business to some and they want to make their mark."

"Ruthless," I agreed. "Maybe we should join a bowling league. No club politics, no fashion; no snobs."

Her face lost every laugh line. "I have limits: no camping, no Motel 6, and no cheap toilet paper. How do you think I'd fit in at the lanes?"

"I don't know," I said. "But I'd pay big money to see it."

Tim practiced with me a couple of times, between the lessons he had started giving at the athletic club. He didn't try to change too much at once. He helped me with my footwork, which he said I needed the most.

"Lynda has one hell of a tough cross court shot," he said. "You'll see."

On the day of our match, I arrived at the tennis club armed with my new Kennex racquet and two lessons under my belt. Lynda was already checked in and warming up with a ball machine. She must have sensed my presence because she stopped and looked my way, completely missing a ball.

"Hey cookie, you ready?" she said. I nodded.

She won the award for the most coordinated and clever outfit. Her crisp white and navy dress had navy lettering on the chest that read, "I CAN'T REMEMBER ALL THOSE THINGS AT ONCE!" The ensemble was completed with white ruffle pants trimmed in navy, a navy visor and navy wristbands. My plain white tennis shorts and ordinary shirt paled by comparison.

"Let's start near the net with short strokes to warm up," she said. "We'll keep moving back as you get comfortable, okay?"

She was fluid and strong. I had speed but no style. Eventually, I forgot about my inability and lack of fashion and just did what I could. After using up half of our court time, she suggested we try a game and I agreed. In fifteen minutes she pounded me 6-1, then 6-2. Actually, I felt good about my slight improvement considering she practiced three days a week and played once a week.

"So it's your social life as well?" I asked.

She nodded. "Not quite as interesting as the boyfriends of a few years ago, but I just don't have an ounce of energy for men anymore. They're so, so ... simple. You know?"

We sat outside under an umbrella and ordered lemonade. She wetted a towel and wiped her face.

"You didn't feel that way about Peter though, did you?" I asked.

She gazed off into the distance and sighed. A smile slowly came over her face. I could almost feel her recollection.

"Peter was everything to me," she said. "He loved me, respected me, thought I was smart and funny ... that only happens once in a lifetime."

We sat for a bit, each lost in our own memories. I usually talked my way out of long silences, but it felt right to let things be.

"I never thought I could trust a man that much—giving him all of my love. But I did. And he smoothed out my rough edges, always forgiving dumb stuff I did. Damn it, I miss him," she said. Tears puddled. "I had it all—someone to love, work I enjoyed with the horses and always something to look forward to."

The deluge of emotion touched me. Feeling guilty for asking about Peter, I reached across the table and took her hand. "I'm so sorry, Lynda, for bringing up old hurts," I said. "I can't even fathom a love like that."

"He showed me a wonderful life and then left me here, alone. I had him for ten years, but you know what, Nancy? That time went so quick, I wish I'd kept a diary. It might sustain me now."

Neither of us spoke. She must have had friends to help her through the time after Peter died. I was ready to ask when she spoke. "If it hadn't been for Nora, I don't know what I would've done. Right after the funeral she gathered up Tim and me and took us to her ranch," she shook her head. "We stayed so long we did laundry three times."

"Tell me about Nora."

She sat up straighter, like there was purpose in what she was about to say. "We met in the horse business, here in Arizona. She was the trainer all the owners wanted. I was a rider, a relative newcomer, but quickly gained recognition on the circuit. Our common ground was the wonder we shared in the strength and beauty of horses. Because of her coaching and nurturing, I became a winner at shows, and I became her much-needed ally to help her cope with her loveless marriage. We were two unlikely successes in a macho world."

She sighed and bent her head down. "We lived so far apart but Nora and Leon would meet up with Peter and me after horse shows. We'd stay in a nice hotel for an extra day and party. Peter could make Leon almost fun. Nora and I were always amazed."

"How often do you see her?" I asked.

Lynda took a gulp of her lemonade. "Now that we're all done with the horses, hardly ever. Her ranch is in southern Arizona, across the border from Mexico. We phone each other, but even that has dropped off. Even so, we are always able to pick up right where we left off."

The layers of new information filled many gaps in my understanding of Lynda's life. Underneath all of the bravado, humor, and sarcasm was tragedy—a real life drama that, up until this moment, I had felt belonged only to me.

"You know, we ought to think about entering some doubles tournaments," she said suddenly, with a grin like the Cheshire cat.

"Uh-oh," I muttered. The idea of serious tennis wasn't in my plan.

"We'll start tomorrow. I'll pay for the pro to look at your game and see where to begin. You can do this. No," she corrected herself, "we can do this."

Eddie wasted no time in assessing my many shortcomings and a suggesting of what to tackle first. Somehow he knew just how far to push and when it had been enough for the day. I couldn't determine his age, but his diplomacy and slightly weathered face hinted late thirties.

"Let's review the three things we worked on today. It would be good if you did drills three times a week for the next two weeks and then we'll re-evaluate. Sound fair?" he said. No smile, no nonsense. His patience won me over.

"I can take instruction," I said. "And Lynda wants me to do this, so I promise I'll give it my all." He nodded. We walked back toward the club. "Am I beyond help?"

"Absolutely you can improve. You'll surprise yourself," Eddie said.

I decided to check out the new clothes Lynda mentioned had arrived at the club earlier that week. A mound of fur on the counter caught my eye as I entered the pro shop. A gorgeous tabby cat sat curled around a member sign-in sheet.

"What a beautiful animal," I said as I petted him.

Connie, the buyer at the club, was unpacking boxes and tagging merchandise.

"That's Prince. He's our club cat," she said. "Some kid named him that because he acts like he owns the place. Just showed up one day a couple years ago and we fed him. Been here ever since."

Prince glanced up at me and bent his head back to my hand for more scratches. I'd never seen such a big cat, except for a Maine coon. Later, when I shared my appreciation for Prince with Lynda, she beamed.

Over the next several weeks, whenever Lynda and I practiced, I arrived early so I'd have time for Prince. He liked to lie beside me with his head in my lap. One day Lynda caught me as I held him to my chest just before putting him back on the counter, his favorite perch.

"You should get an animal for company," she said.

I stroked Prince once last time. "That was Tim's opinion too," I said.

Robin's two-week summer visit was on the horizon, even though it had been postponed to July. I still hadn't even mentioned anything about Tim to her. Maybe she would take it better if he lived in my house, like an extension of family instead of boyfriend. I mentioned this thought to Lynda one day after our tennis practice.

"Lynda, how would you feel about Tim moving in with me? Just for the summer," I asked. "He mentioned that he and Brian will be giving up their apartment as soon as the semester ended."

She raised an eyebrow and then smiled. "That would be wonderful. And he's there all the time anyhow."

I told her that I hadn't suggested it to Tim yet—that I wanted her approval first. She came around the breakfast table and hugged me hard.

"You are good for each other," she said. "I don't know how long it will last but I see how happy you both are."

On move-in day Tim came with wonderful male toys: a state-of-the-art sound system, a reel-to-reel tape player, a large Sony television, and a Weber barbeque. We soon settled into a routine, and I phoned Robin to disclose the new living arrangement.

"Tim has moved in for the summer," I said without taking a breath. She said nothing. "He will be able to help me with house chores and take you places if I'm at work."

"What if we don't like him being there?"

"Let's give it a chance, okay?" I said. "Will you do that for me?" Very slowly, she said yes.

I emphasized Tim's good points, but Robin quieted each time I brought up his name. In the following weeks she usually started conversations with, "Is that Tim guy still there?"

On the other hand, my office pals were anxious to meet the boy toy, as they nicknamed him. We were invited to a number of social events, but I wasn't ready for the scrutiny. Still, a week after Tim moved in, I agreed to bring him to a couples' function, though I knew everyone would be at least ten years older than he. The night we strolled into the Arizona Biltmore I had butterflies up the wazoo. I struggled with Tim to get him to dress down. Reluctantly, he wore jeans and a golf shirt—a combination as foreign to him as an American car.

Conversation quieted the minute we walked into the Cholla Room. Heads turned and fifty pair of eyes judged us. Men resumed their conversations but many of the women continued to stare at Tim. His teen idol good looks made him reek of sex. He was cordial to the women, but eventually he headed toward the bar where the men congregated.

The guys held back and seemed to close him out of their conversations by talking about work, children, or a distant sports team. They didn't want a young stud in their group. My back was to them while I faked a conversation with two wives, listening to the men all the while. It irritated me that my pals were being such jerks. Before I left the wives, a new salesman asked Tim, "So, what do you do?"

"I go to ASU," Tim said. You could have heard a pin drop. "It's hell, but it beats selling copy machines."

They all laughed. The ice cracked. The conversation then turned to ASU football, a subject that had no age barrier. I tuned out.

The rest of the party went like any other. That is, until the end of the night when the office tramp, Helena, circled a group of women where Tim was embedded, then snaked her way in and said, drunkedly, "Give me your best kiss, you gorgeous hunk. I see no reason why Nancy should have all the fun."

Quickly the men cheered. All eyes were on Tim and Helena. He put an arm lightly around her waist and gave her a lengthy French job. They parted amidst cat calls. Helena patted his butt. My neck and face flushed. I wanted to punch the crap out of both of them. Everyone watched for my reaction, but I laughed as big as I could with all the others.

At the end of the party we drove off the hotel grounds in silence.

I glared ten thousand icy daggers at him. He must have felt them because he suddenly looked over. "What?" he said. "Something wrong?"

"Are you out of your mind? You don't have a single clue why I'm mad?"

He stopped for a red light and messed with the radio station. "No. You didn't have fun?" It didn't seem possible that the guy I thought I knew had done such a thing. There was no explanation. My temper was on the rampage.

"Tim, my god, you French kissed the office tramp," I screamed. "Are you so caught up in your own ego that you need to know women want you?"

He held up a hand to signal enough. "Okay, okay. So I kissed the office slut. Ilene, Arlene, whatever. Who cares? It was nothing. No thing. Got it?"

The rest of ride was silent save for an occasional throat clearing and the whir of the air conditioner. I wondered what my pals were saying and felt humiliated.

He is a kid. And it finally showed up. What did you expect?

We got to the house, undressed, and fell into bed back-to-back without a word. Tim sighed. I pretended to be asleep. Every minute felt like an hour.

Tim brushed my leg. "I'm sorry. It was dumb. I only wanted to fit in with your friends. Please forgive me. Please?" He then gently massaged my shoulders. I rolled over to face him. "You embarrassed the hell out of me," I said.

"I was wrong," he said. "I know not what I do."

The week before Robin arrived, Lynda called me at work. "Is everything okay?" I said, surprised and confused. She laughed briefly.

"I guess this will sound stupid to you, but there's a problem at the racquet club. The place has been sold, and the new owner showed up today. He hates cats and said to take Prince to the pound. Can you believe it? I'm so upset I don't know what to do," she said. I remained silent. She out-waited me.

"That's terrible," I said, scooting my chair closer to the desk, "But how does this have anything to do with me?"

"You said you were thinking of getting a pet," she said.

"No, you and Tim said I should get a pet ... maybe even a cat."

"I stand corrected," she conceded. "But you've seen Prince. He's such a lover, he's trained and neutered. I saw to that."

"Lynda, I'm gone all day. Tim will be giving tennis lessons at the club, Robin is due. It's too much," I said.

She sighed. "Prince is accustomed to being outside for long periods. He's independent and lovable—perfect for you. Come out today and we'll have lunch."

This woman was a match for me. She usually got her way. When all else failed, she threw in a free meal. I felt beaten.

I caved. "Okay, I will come for lunch. But there's no firm commitment about anything else. Agreed?"

When I got to the club, I found Lynda at the sign-in desk. Prince occupied his usual spot with his head half-tucked under one paw. His coloring was gray with stripes, and he had a thick band of white down his chest. The white continued up to his face, circling his eyes and nose making him look like a bandit. I stroked him and he rubbed against me. He hooked me with his magnificent green eyes and mewed. I picked him up. I needed both hands to lift him from his regal perch. He cradled himself in my arms, and I carried him outside. Lynda followed at my heels. She knew how I felt before I did.

"The owner says we have to find a home for him before six tonight or he's taking matters into his own hands," she said with her head down. The three of us sat there for a while. She put a hand on mine.

"I know this is a big deal for you, but he's great, right?" she said. "Handsome and loving. Like you, cookie."

"Lynda, I don't know who's the better con man, you or the cat," I said. "Okay, I'll take him."

She stood abruptly and walked over to her car, where she opened the trunk and took out a grocery bag and a pet carrier. I shrugged my shoulders as if to say what's up?

"Supplies for Prince: bowls, cat toys, liter box, and food. Just in case you said yes today, I didn't think you'd have time to shop," she said. "And you'll need the carrier to take him in the car. In fact, let's do it right now."

Getting Prince into the carrier was an ordeal. Gentle pushes gave way to firmness. Not happy about his new quarters, he dug deep for earthy, guttural noises, like he was practicing to be a lion. Lynda said she'd follow me to my house—"just in case." I had no idea what she meant.

Once inside the house with all the paraphernalia, I opened the carrier and Prince leaped out. He ran the full length of the house several times and continued making weird noises. He jumped over furniture, made erratic moves around the table and changed direction several times. He scratched at the carpet and leaped up on the back of the sofa. For just a minute or so he surveyed the room from this higher plateau.

I plopped down and shook my head in disbelief. Lynda moved to the floor and watched Prince continue his prowling. She held a hand out and waited. In no time, Prince ended up in her lap. She petted him. He purred and twitched his tail from side to side.

"How do you know what to do with him?" I asked.

She shrugged. "Don't know. Animals are easy for me, unlike children and mothers."

In the ensuing silence, I wondered what made me think I could possibly be a good mother to a cat when I still felt inadequate with Robin.

Lynda picked up Prince and moved to the couch beside me. She held him as if he were a baby. It tickled me.

"You seem like a great mother," I said. "And Tim sure thinks the world of you."

"He and I are both a little off. The other two sons wouldn't agree with Timothy," she said. "There is another side to this mother thing, you know."

I arched a brow and leaned forward to scratch Prince's head.

"For example, as much as you say your mother did you wrong I'll bet you chastised her. Said she was out-of-date or old-fashioned. Got mad because she didn't see your point of view. Right?" Sweat broke out on my neck.

"So your mother isn't president of your fan club," Lynda continued. "It's really not her job. At least, I don't think so. Children need discipline, guidance and love. It sounds to me like she gave you all three but you are pissed about the discipline, maybe. Even the best children are like pianos— they need tuning." She poked my knee. "That includes you, cookie."

Prince curled himself into a ball between us. He would be good for me. Lynda sat back and pulled her legs underneath her. "Now my mother, Marie, is truly a witch. She never planned to have more than one child, which made me the unwelcome second. Just a taste of what I mean: my mother testified against me in my divorce proceedings against Dave. Under oath, she said I either caused his infidelity or I lied about it."

I gaped, unable to think of anything to say. Her bad mother story more than trumped mine. The cruelty was beyond my comprehension.

Lynda set her jaw firmly. Her cheek muscles tensed. "The irony is I am the one footing the bill for her nursing home. As mean as she is, I'm sure she could live ten more years. But whatever it is, it's taking too long."

Daily life resumed. Prince became the pet extraordinaire, roaming outside while I worked. Tim gave lessons at the club, had tennis practice every day, did the grocery shopping and meal preparations, mowed the lawn, and kept the cars clean. He extended thoughtfulness in cards, notes in my car or planner, unexpected flowers, a small gift of special bath powder or chocolate. I felt like a princess.

Lynda also found cards for me, although they were quite different from Tim's. Hers were irreverent. The more time I spent with her, the more I appreciated her. Through her reasoning, she continued to bridge the murky water that separated my mother and me. I baked her muffins, cookies, and banana bread. She loved sweet things more than she liked to admit, and she made such a fuss it made me want to do more. It was fun to show up at her door unannounced before I went to work.

"You dahling girl, come right in," she'd say, and welcome me with a cup of her strong coffee. She and I were both morning people—rising early to exercise and read the paper. Tim got up late and slightly grumpy.

One morning at her house, I proposed a plan.

"What would you think about a dinner for all of us, your whole family with their spouses?" I said.

Lynda put her coffee cup down and rubbed her forehead. "Oh honey, I don't know. It's such a weird group," she sighed.

We sat and watched Ralph chase a rabbit around the pool. Somehow a cocker spaniel didn't suit Lynda; she seemed more like a big-dog person.

"We could all get together for Tim's birthday," she said slowly. She posed it more as an idea, at first, rather than something she was really considering. "Yeah, at El Chorro," she continued, sounding more inspired. "It would be safe if we have it at a restaurant. Everyone will be on their best behavior."

"Excellent. So fill me in on the details," I said. Though Tim had already described his family to me, I wanted to hear Lynda's take on them. "I know that everyone thinks their family is straight out of a comic book, but I'm sure they're normal guys. You might just be a little critical, yourself."

She giggled. "Sure. Well, John is tall and quiet. He is conservative and slow to warm up. A little aloof, in an accountant sort of way. He's been married many times, since he likes to be the rescuer. Then there's Todd, who Tim calls Psycho-man. He's short, with a slight build, ambitious but a bit of a temper issue. He's strange in places. I have to give him credit, though—he has done well with his landscaping business and investing his money."

"See, sounds like any other family. Everyone is different," I said.

On the evening of the party, Tim and I picked up Lynda. Dusk had brought the temperature back down into the high nineties, and there was even a slight breeze. The blue sky was punched at the horizon with brilliant bursts of red and orange.

We arrived at El Chorro promptly at six. The old adobe restaurant had been a mainstay since the forties with its white-washed walls and dark beamed overhangs. Blue and white handmade tiles accented arched doorways and countertops.

John and his wife Janet waited at a large round table. He was attractive in exactly the way Lynda had described. Janet didn't shield her boredom as she yawned during Lynda's introductions. She took a drag off her cigarette and sipped a martini. Todd arrived right after us with his girlfriend, Donna, lagging behind.

A round of drinks supported by a generous assortment of appetizers got us through the first thirty minutes. I noticed Lynda checking her watch.

Why did I want to do this? It's worse than work.

Tim and I sat closest to Lynda. Momentarily I forgot we were supposed to be celebrating Tim's birthday, since the gathering felt like forced togetherness—nothing happy or party-like about it. Lynda and Tim tried to engage Janet and John while I swallowed and attempted the same with Todd. Eventually though, I hit a gold mine when I asked about his business.

"My challenges boil down to two issues: long hours of manual work which I believe I need to do along with the crew, and the other is finding reliable minimum-wage employees. The men are mostly Hispanic," Todd said.

Donna watched his every word but never said anything. I focused on her, finally, and asked her what she did. Todd inched forward and said, "She's a secretary."

I did not like his answering for her and assumed Donna didn't either. "Where do you work?" I asked. "I'm always amazed at the roles a secretary has to juggle."

Donna smiled, her shoulders fell, and she glanced at Todd. "I keep telling her she needs to get a higher-paying job," he said. She nodded. I turned back to him, since my plan to include her wasn't working.

"Lynda says your business is quite successful, so you must have found ways to overcome the obstacles," I said as I passed some of the appetizers around.

"True," he said and sat up straighter. "I speak Spanish, that's a big help. And I provide coffee, juice, and doughnuts every morning before we start work. Plus I always buy lunch for everyone. The food thing has worked better than anything else I've tried." His eyes shifted all around the table.

"Great idea," I said.

"You still have to let them know who's boss," he said. His jaw muscles quivered as he spoke.

After dinner, Tim opened his tacky birthday cards. Out of nowhere, an enormous baked Alaska arrived at the table. We all oohed and aahed. Tim blew out the candles and winked at me.

As soon as everyone had taken a piece, Todd stood up. "I have an announcement."

Lynda stopped with her forkful of dessert in midair.

He shifted his weight and dug his hands in his pockets. "Someone has offered to buy my business. It's more than a fair price. Plus I want to move to California."

Lynda glanced around the table at the rest of us. "But then what will you do? You have no education or training in anything else."

Todd's arms crossed over his chest. "I don't know what I'll do. But I'm not stupid. I'll figure out something. It won't happen soon enough for me."

Lynda leaned across the table and lowered her voice. "You've spent eight years building up this business. And why California, for heaven's sake?"

Todd stepped back so fast his chair fell over. "What's it to you? Or anyone else here? You're all just out for yourselves. Then there's Tim with his trust fund from Peter. I'm sick to death of the whole scene. C'mon Donna."

They were out of sight before anyone spoke. We all stared at each other trying to make sense of what had just happened. Even Janet participated.

Nothing like a little drama to glue a family together.

Lynda slowly eased back into her chair. She looked at each of us and said, "I think we should all bow our heads in a moment of silence for the state of California."

It was over 110 degrees when Robin arrived. On the phone, I had down-played the heat with talk about the club pool, all the newly added activities at the day camp she'd be returning to, and her friend Tracy, who lived next door. All of my preparation for her to meet Tim seemed in vain.

"The kid is only twelve years younger than me," he'd said. "There won't be a problem. We'll hit it off great."

Despite his assurances, I paced at the gate waiting for Robin's American Airlines flight. When she emerged, she smiled and waved, and I felt a lump in my throat. She was taller, thinner, with short hair. We hugged and hugged.

"Boy, it's really hot," she said when we walked outside. "We need to get to the pool." A few people standing nearby laughed.

I had planned that, when Robin arrived, we would have a full afternoon together before she met Tim. I had kept Prince a secret knowing how much she loved cats and that discovering him would delight her. I was right; Robin eeked when she saw him. Prince ran straight toward her. She picked him up with both hands but his behind still hung low. His face drooped over one arm as he gave me the most pained expression.

"What a great big pig poody tat you are," she said as she held him in her arms. She kissed his neck and smiled at me. "I love him, Mom. I didn't know you liked cats."

"I don't," I said. "But him, I love!"

We put Robin's things away and headed out the door to pick up Tracy and head for the Arizona Athletic Club. The girls giggled and whispered to each other in the back seat.

The club was empty at three in the afternoon. It took us no time to claim the Olympic-size pool for ourselves, where we spent afternoon playing—Marco Polo, doing cannonballs, and racing from one end of the pool to the other.

We got back to the house thirty minutes before Tim arrived. Robin sat on a stool at the kitchen counter and told me about school in Ohio while I made spinach manicotti for supper. She stopped mid-sentence when Tim walked in.

"Hey Robin, nice to meet you. I've heard a lot of good things about you from your mom," he said as he took a stool beside her and tried to give her a quick hug. She stiffened. "So, how was your trip?"

"Okay," she said barely aloud and looked around for the cat.

"How long does it take to fly from Ohio?" he asked, his voice slightly affected.

She shrugged her shoulders. "I dunno. We stopped in St. Louis."

It was agonizing. I tried to rescue the situation for both of them. "Robin, why don't you tell Tim about the camping trip your Girl Scout troop took this summer?"

Robin continued to eye him. "Do you camp?"

"That would be Motel 6," he said and laughed.

She frowned. "Huh?"

Things did not improve. Tim ate his dinner and then retreated to the living room and the television. Robin let Prince out in the backyard and then followed him around. I heard her calling, "Here kitty, kitty," every so often.

"Can Prince sleep with me?" Robin asked as she headed for bed. I warned her that Prince probably wouldn't stay there all night. He circled for a while before he curled up against her legs. Even though it was only eight o'clock, a day full of worry about Robin meeting Tim and the heat had drained me.

I collapsed on the couch. Tim gave me an affectionate hug, and then returned his attention to the TV.

"She's cute," he said. "Just a little spoiled."

It shocked me. "You can't mean that."

"Well, she's used to having you all to herself. This will be an adjustment for all of us."

I took a week of vacation from work and gave her all my attention. We played games, swam at the club, and saw movies. Tracy spent the better part of each day with us. One day I heard contagious giggles from the backyard. The girls had dressed Prince in doll clothes and were pushing him around in a little buggy. I never saw a sadder expression on an animal's face.

I bragged to Robin about Lynda's pool with the swim-up bar. She begged to see it as soon as possible. I had not witnessed Lynda with children but I knew her less-than-enthusiastic views about them. Although it didn't worry me, I was curious to find out how it would go. The first day at Lynda's, Robin disappeared around the corner of the house to see where the pool ended. She ran back, wide-eyed, and grabbed Lynda by the hand.

"Wow. Wow. So neat. Can I go in right now—Mrs. B?" she said.

Lynda nodded. "Yes, cookie II. But you must call me Lynda."

Robin swam and splashed. She talked Lynda into throwing quarters into the deep end so she could retrieve them. Lynda and I were in the middle of a conversation when Robin yelled, "Oh waitress, can I order now?" She sat perched on one of the stools at the swim-up bar.

Lynda laughed and disappeared into the house. She came out wearing an apron and carrying a pad. A pencil stuck out of hair. She stepped down into the pit so she was even with Robin.

"Okay, cookie II. What's your pleasure? And hurry it up, I've got five tables," Lynda said.

I enjoyed the show, sitting on the sidelines and smiling.

Robin leaned on her elbows. "I'll have a cheeseburger, fries, and a coke."

Lynda shook her head. "Sorry. All out."

"How about a grilled cheese and potato chips?"

Lynda smiled. "Yes to the chips, no to the grilled cheese. Between the hours of two and four the chef cleans the grill."

Robin scratched her head and kicked up water around her legs. "Peanut butter and jelly?"

"Excellent choice," Lynda said. "I'll be right back with your order."

We all laughed. The rest of the afternoon went faster than a day at the county fair. Watching Lynda and Robin banter back and forth delighted me the most.

"Thank you Lynda," Robin said. "Can I come again tomorrow? I'll bring my Karen Carpenter tape."

Lynda nodded. "As long as you bring your mother."

That night I told Tim about the day and the fun Robin had with Lynda. He didn't seem surprised. "Ma would accept anyone who belongs to you," he mumbled without looking up from his newspaper.

After Robin returned to Ohio, we settled back into what remained of our summer. Sometimes Tim discussed investment strategy with Lynda, which always led to a debate. Lynda had a conservative approach while Tim wanted big gains and talked about his dreams. He claimed he could afford to take risks and Lynda countered that his trust fund could give him a leg up for the future.

"Tim," I said. "What was that remark that Todd made at your birthday party about your trust fund? Not that it's any of my business."

I chopped onions for his spaghetti sauce while he sautéed mushrooms. He stopped for a moment and turned to me. "Peter had a certain amount in his will that was released to me on my eighteenth birthday. No doubt my brothers are resentful because he didn't do the same for them."

Ahhhh. So much makes sense.

The mushrooms hissed behind him. He grabbed a spoon and stirred. I sat down at the counter.

"All the debates between Lynda and me are about what to do with the money. How to make it grow, how to protect it, what to invest in—that's why we talk about it so much. Right now it's sitting in the bank," he said.

"Is that how you bought your car?" I asked. He scowled and kept his head down.

Bingo. Hit a nerve.

"You know the answer," he said. "Lynda had a cow. I told her it was an investment. And I believe it. Sometimes she treats me like I'm a kid. To tell you the truth, I think she's still pissed that Peter left me the money. Or maybe she was mad because she didn't know it was in the will. At least, not until the lawyer told her, after Peter died."

Once Lynda was displeased about something, she was like a freight train at full throttle. Everything about what Peter did went against her better judgment. Youth and money could be a lethal combination, with Tim just an innocent recipient. He did, however, seem worldly and experienced to me. He had traveled often: overseas, to all the top U.S. cities, Bermuda, Hawaii—all places I had only dreamed about.

"I've been to New York," I said once. He laughed, thinking I was joking.

It wasn't too long before Tim made his investment decision. Neither conservative nor risky, but worse. Tim invested one hundred thousand dollars with a friend's father who was a pie-in-the-sky inventor, a genius of a man with hare-brained ideas that were never well executed. I met him once and didn't think he was dishonest, just incapable of putting all the pieces together. The engineer dreamed of the day one of his patents would take the family to the rich side of town and away from their cramped tract house that had been built in the fifties. I couldn't believe it when Tim reported the news with all the excitement of a kid who had just made the little league team.

"Mr. Munroe let me be one of the five investors. Me. I own twenty percent of the action," Tim said. "My investment will make me a million in four years."

Stay calm. Maybe this is the one. Just because all the other ones didn't work out.

"What is it, exactly?" I said.

"Mr. M. invented a machine that will make it profitable to mine gold from small veins ... like a giant grinder-sifter. In the past, miners excavated the large veins and left the rest behind. There are hundreds of abandoned mines all over Ecuador," he said. "He identified the largest mine and secured a lease where the dredging will start next week."

I worried over Lynda's reaction. It wasn't just the investment but with whom and the amount. She didn't mince words once she made up her mind about someone, and she had made derogatory remarks about Munroe in the past.

"What does Lynda think about this?" I said sounding as blasé as possible.

"She doesn't know a thing," he said. "I'll have to tell her Munroe doesn't have a slot left for her."

It was hard not to laugh. Then again, it was hard not to cry. Lynda would go ballistic. I took a deep breath. "I think you should tell her. It is a lot of money."

"My money," he said and stiffened up.

Lynda took the news better than I thought, since Tim remained alive. She fumed and swore for several hours and then stomped out of my house. When Tim wasn't watching she shrugged her shoulders, probably out of exasperation.

"This calls for a celebration," Tim said to me. "The beginning of a whole new future. Let's go out to La Chaumire, I have one more surprise."

It seemed like a good diversion. The part about one more surprise didn't register. I wanted anything to get my mind off the craziness of his scheme. I agreed with Lynda. The chances of Mr. M. pulling off this venture sounded like less than a pipe dream—this time it sounded like a scam.

Tim mentioned again that there was one more surprise. "Get dressed up," he said with a big grin.

La Chaumire was tucked on a quiet street. The charming cottage, converted to a restaurant, looked like it had been lifted from France and plunked down in old Scottsdale years before. Hanging floral baskets and mature shrubbery added to the quaintness. The maitre d ushered us to a quiet table overlooking the gardens. Tim ordered champagne.

"This investment thing isn't just for me," Tim said. "It's for us. For the future."

I squirmed in my seat. His eyes stayed focused on me. He reached for my hand and stroked it. The night, the attention, was over the top, and I couldn't get comfortable. If other patrons had been in the room, I'm sure they would have stared and wondered what in the heck was going on.

Tim reached into his sport coat and pulled out a velvet box. He set it on table. "Nancy," he said. "I've never met anyone like you. Never. And I know it's only been a few months, but I want to marry you. Will you marry me?"

As he talked, he opened the box to reveal a huge pear-shaped diamond. Movie star big.

"Oh no," I said. Nothing registered. I did care for him, he was fun, I'd had attention and love thrown upon me, but it wasn't right. We weren't a fit. He had stunned me beyond the ability to react, except to say, "I can't."

Tim smiled and slid the ring on my finger. "You can't marry me or you can't wear the ring?"

It fit perfectly and sparkled every time I moved my hand. "I can't make a decision about marriage. It's all too much. Too soon," I said.

Tim rested his elbows on the table and watched me admire the ring. "How about if you just wear the ring for now and think about the other? I want a partner, a lover ... I don't want to lose you, and I feel if I don't act soon, you'll be gone."

The next day at the office, no one said a word. Even though they couldn't help but notice the rock there were no congratulations, no hugs, no comments, no questions. One of the secretaries jokingly asked if it was real.

I went home early. The dishwasher needed unloading, and Prince wanted attention. Resolution to his proposal was necessary. Chores did not solve my problem. I got in the car and headed for Lynda's.

She answered the door after several rings. It's possible she may have expected a Jehovah's Witness or a Mormon on a mission. She claimed both visited her so often that there must be a conspiracy.

"Nancy dear. What a wonderful surprise. And in the middle of the day," she said and opened the door wider. "Come on in."

I followed her into the kitchen and plopped down at the table. She sat across from me.

"What in the world is it? You look absolutely distraught," she said.

"Lynda, look at this," I said and drew my hand up from under the table. The ring sparkled in the partial sunlight.

She gasped and then smiled. "Oh my god. You're engaged to Tim? When did this happen?"

My shoulders slumped and I exhaled. "Last night. It is so bizarre. He did ask me to marry him, but I didn't answer. He wants me to wear the ring and think about it. It's nuts. But here I am wearing the ring."

Lynda poured iced tea. She waited for me to talk but I had nothing to say. The silence comforted me somehow. She reached across and held my hand.

"You'll know what to do. Timothy for all of his maturity is still a puppy. A very romantic puppy," she said.

She didn't say a word about the size of the diamond or even hint at what an extravagance it was. In a way, that disappointed me. How much had it cost? And right after the gold mine investment? How much did he have, anyhow?

Tim paced when he learned I had gone to see Lynda without him. He claimed he'd wanted to make the announcement.

"Tim, there is no announcement. All of this is too much for me," I said.

"The money you're spending and how quickly everything is moving is making me very uncomfortable. Then there's Robin to consider."

We sat on the couch without looking at each other. He cracked his knuckles and fiddled with a stack of magazines on the coffee table. I wanted diversion. Tim might have felt it too because he suggested we invite Lynda over for steaks. It was the perfect break.

Lynda's presence soothed my uneasiness. We enjoyed a delicious dinner and a good bottle of wine. Things could certainly be worse. No one mentioned a thing about the ring or anything related to it. I relaxed for the first time.

"Nancy, I wonder if you'd have any interest in a tennis tournament with me next weekend in Tucson," Lynda said. "I think you've really come a long way, and it would be fun. Just the two of us, my treat. That would be okay with you Tim, yes?"

Tim nodded and all eyes concentrated on me. A break sounded more than good. Forgetting the tennis, just to get out of town. Maybe Lynda would provide some insight to my dilemma. Someone somewhere must be able to see the way out of the jungle I had created.

"Love to, love to," I said. "Can't promise how good the tennis will be, but it sounds like fun. I can't even remember the last girl trip I had."

"And I need to start planning my schedule for senior year," Tim said. "Plus someone needs to look after Prince."

The cat peeked up at us at the mention of his name. He was such a smart guy. I reached down and lifted him up into my lap.

I had heard a lot of good things about Westward Look Resort in Tucson. It was originally built in 1912, as an elegant private hacienda. In the early 1920s, the owners expanded it into a small inn with fifteen casitas, still maintaining the ranch feel. Over the years there was plenty of room for expansion on the 172 acres, nestled into the Catalina Mountains. The casitas surrounded the main building, which had a restaurant, pro shop, tennis courts and pool, and a patio with a 180-degree view of the city to the south. Lynda said that she and Peter had stayed there many times, even once with Nora and Leon, but that she hadn't been back after Peter died. I worried momentarily that it could be sad for her, but that concern faded as we came up the long drive to the lobby. She pointed out various landmarks and perked up the closer we got. "Oh boy, oh boy. I'm ready for some fun. How about you, Nancy?"

We checked in and made a beeline for our room. After all, it was cocktail time and we were both parched after the two-hour drive from Phoenix. We showered and put on our best sundresses.

Music and conversation wafted from the bar. A very sexy guitar player sat elevated in the middle of things. We decided to sit halfway back so we could talk but still hear the music. Our waitress said the guitarist's name was Carlos. He had the whole Latino thing going: coal-black hair pulled back into a ponytail, worn black leather hat, white ruffled shirt open one too many buttons, mariachi-style pants and black boots. All of that added to his chiseled face and magnetic black eyes that danced when he smiled. His looks were just the beginning. He could sing. Every woman in the place thought he sang to her, and he had their rapt attention from the first song. Lynda and I sat back, finally, and enjoyed our icy margaritas and the scenery. All of it.

"Here's to us, cookie, and our upcoming victory," she said. We clinked glasses.

An hour or so passed and I began to think that Carlos was flirting with me but I quickly realized it wasn't me his eyes rested on; it was Lynda. Carlos asked if anyone had a request. No one spoke. Finally Lynda glanced out over the patio to give anyone else a last chance to speak up. "How about 'Por un Amor'?" she said.

Carlos smiled. He strummed a few bars. "*Si, senora. Por favor*, will you join me?"

Lynda let out an embarrassed laugh but joined him on the small stage with encouraging applause from many. Her gutsy move shocked me. I knew she spoke some Spanish, but I had no idea she could sing. And sing she did, from the soles of her feet. They flirted with each other during the whole number as if they had sung it together many times. People stopped talking and watched. They sang to the audience, to one another, to me. I stood and clapped, wolf-whistled, and whooped it up. Others followed my example.

Lynda was exhausted and reeling from performance adrenaline. I hugged her and helped her into her seat. "How great was that?" I said. "I had no idea you could sing … and in Spanish. You fox."

She let herself melt into the chair. Her cheeks and neck flushed as she gasped, "I wasn't sure I could do it but I decided what the hell. I needed an adventure. Besides, I don't know any of these people. I was terrified at first, all those eyes staring at me. What fun. I loved it."

"And everyone loved watching you."

She gulped a glass of water. "We do have a tennis match at seven. I mean, I'd love to have dinner and then Carlos but I think I better settle for dinner."

Eventually we gathered our things and stood as Lynda blew a kiss to Carlos. He put his hand in the air to catch it and winked at her. Lynda and I walked arm-in-arm toward the dining room. She shook her head.

"What?" I said.

"Oh nothing," she said softly.

The next morning came fast. After a light breakfast, and dressed like we were due on Wimbledon Center Court, Lynda and I headed for our first match. The cloudless blue sky and a good night's sleep gave us reason to smile. We giggled over the memory of the night before.

We volleyed for fifteen minutes and then went through our standard warm-up routine. Other courts filled up and matches began. Still our opponents didn't show. Lynda headed for the pro shop to investigate. She returned with a Carol Channing grin. "We have won our first match by default, cookie. The pro said we will play the winner of the match on court 2. Shall we have a look?"

Our victims smacked the ball back and forth. There was little conversation and no dawdling. Battle lines were drawn, and it was easy to see both wanted victory. Neither of us spoke as we assessed their ability. My stomach churned. Determination and perseverance would not be enough.

I prayed silently for courage and not to humiliate myself. The match went on for another hour, only to end with a tie-breaker. Maybe we'd have the stamina advantage.

We introduced ourselves to Rhonda and Suzanne, each probably in their early forties. Rhonda was an over-tanned, bleached blonde with tons of gold bracelets and necklaces. I hoped that all the jewelry would add to her fatigue. They took the first game handily and we changed sides. Lynda gave me a pep talk. It helped because we won the next two games, and then the trouble started. Rhonda called two of Lynda's shots out although they were both inside the line. Lynda let the first one go, but the second time she approached the net and asked Rhonda to do the same. I couldn't hear the whole thing but it was something like, "Listen Goldilocks—that's just plain bullshit. You don't need to cheat to beat us, and you know it. One more call like that and I'll stop and file a complaint. You have no idea who you're dealing with."

Lynda fumed as she resumed her spot and said to me, "I put the bitch on notice."

Goldilocks, aka Rhonda, never said another word. Lynda held serve and we were off to an early lead before the wheels fell off. Suffice to say, in the end our victory plans were short-lived before they were squashed completely.

We met Rhonda and Suzanne at the net to congratulate them and shake hands. Rhonda invited us for margaritas, which I thought was a surprising display of sportsmanship. I opened my mouth to accept when Lynda declined by saying we had other plans.

Once we were out of earshot I said, "What plans, Lynda? I don't remember you saying anything about that."

She laughed. "Oh cookie, you're too much. I just couldn't take being with them another minute. It's possible, very possible that I'm a sore loser."

Lynda insisted I drive her Pontiac Firebird home. Her back bothered her; I had seen her down a few pills before we played and again afterwards.

I had planned to talk with her about Tim and the ring but it didn't happen. Not until we were twenty miles from home and all the worry reappeared to welcome me.

"What do you think you'll do?" Lynda said. "About a wedding and all that other stuff."

I coughed nervously while I stalled for a reply. "The whole thing has unnerved me. He's cute and sweet to me, but he's so young. Half the time I wonder what in the heck is going on in my brain. And the rest of the time I enjoy the attention, the love, the companionship. But we're not on the same page. If it were the right decision it should be easy. There can't be doubts in the beginning." She patted my shoulder, "You're a good girl. I know you'll do what's best for both of you. And no matter what, I'll always love you. You and that big cat of yours."

Tim wrestled with the cannelloni and stuffing as I told him about the weekend. It came out as a short version of all the activities. Somehow the tale of Carlos didn't make the cut and neither did the talks about my uneasiness over the ring and possible engagement. I wanted to get things out in the open but reconsidered. Maybe later. Maybe tomorrow.

After dinner I reviewed my plan for new business and Tim wanted to go to the athletic club to meet up with a friend.

"I'll be home by nine or so," he said as he left.

The quiet house allowed me to focus on how to get back into the groove as a leader in the office. It became apparent I hadn't been submitting enough proposals for new accounts. I also needed to schedule more product demonstrations. People needed to actually see what the machines could do and how purchasing one would save them time.

Prince wandered into the dining room where I'd spread out my planner and lists of potential clients. He lay on the carpet and occasionally peered up at me. I was so grateful to have the time to myself that I lost track of the hour. When Prince stood at the back door and meowed, I noticed it was after ten o'clock. I wasn't concerned since I knew where Tim had gone.

Washing and ironing used up another hour and made me feel accomplished. I loved to be caught up on household chores and have my week at the office all mapped out.

The Arizona Athletic Club closed at eleven. I assumed Tim would be home at any time. It didn't happen. At midnight I drove over to the club and found the parking lot empty.

It was a restless night. No sleep. Anger. At six I got up and went for my daily three-mile run. Still no Tim. By 7:30 a.m. I had showered and dressed. Once outside, I saw Tim's car parked on the street in front of the house.

What the heck?

I approached the car and found him asleep with the driver's seat reclined as far back as it would go. I swung the door open and scared him.

"What are you doing?" I said. "And where in the hell were you?" His eyes were bloodshot, and he smelled like stale liquor.

"Not so loud," he said. "Things got a little out of hand last night."

I slammed the car door and headed for the house. He stumbled out of his BMW and followed me.

"Hey, wait up. I can explain everything," he said.

No explanation would satisfy me. I was a business-woman with a career living in playland. The predicament should not have surprised me.

He's a kid. You are living with a kid.

I was so far past anger I shook with rage. Going to work was the quickest way to get out of the situation. Just before I got to Phoenix, I took off the diamond and put it in my purse.

The office looked like heaven. I considered kneeling down and kissing the floor. Things were much the same there day after day. I knew what to expect, and it never felt better to be there than that day. I stayed busy all morning and took time to have lunch with the guys. When I said I'd join them, two guys raised their eyebrows at each other but I pretended not to see it. It had been weeks since I'd done that. After lunch, I decided to visit some of my best customers. That always put me in good spirits and quite often resulted in further business. Toward the end of the afternoon, I returned to the office and practiced a new demonstration on one of our hottest copiers. When there was nothing left to delay my return home, I headed home to Tempe.

Tim stayed gone for two days. No phone calls either. I worked my way through all stages of anger, almost the same as dealing with grief. By the time I saw him, I had made my decision. He probably thought he'd give me an opportunity to cool off and then we would kiss and make up. I stared him down once he appeared.

"This isn't some snit," I said.

He frowned and dropped his outstretched arms against his legs. "Hey, c'mon. I got involved in too much fun with my pals. I didn't do anything bad."

"I don't know that. Besides, you were drunk on your ass. And you drove home? I'm thirty-two, a business-woman and mother. I want no part of this."

The diamond glistened as I held it out to Tim. He dropped his head and sat on the floor.

"It won't work. You have growing up to do, and I'm already grown. I can't help you, Tim. I need an equal," I said. His eyes filled up, and tears fell.

I sighed. It wouldn't change my mind, though I felt sorry for him. He had lost his father so young and still wasn't really over it. All of his crazy dreams, his lack of direction, the money—which I now believed could destroy him.

Prince drifted over to me. I picked him up and sat next to Tim. I put an arm around his shoulder. "You were so good to me. Generous and loving, but you should have someone your own age. Someone you can build a whole future with. I already have a child and a career. It's too much of a head start," I said.

He wiped his eyes and took the ring. "It looked good on your finger. What's a guy to do with a used engagement ring?"

The next weekend, Tim and his brother John moved all of his things back to the apartment he had shared with his friend. We tried to talk but it stalled several times. Finally, I went outside and worked on a crossword puzzle while the two of them finished loading his belongings. We mumbled brief goodbyes. I stood in the driveway and watched until they were out of sight.

What a wild six months. Hope I'm never that stupid again.

I staggered back into the house just in time to have privacy as the tears began. I cried so hard my hair hurt. I wasn't clear what I was crying about. I wondered whether people would say, "Well, I could have told you that would happen. What did you expect?" I'd never had so much attention and affection. I'd gotten used to it. I liked it. And then in a flash, it ended.

I threw myself on the bed and lingered in self-pity a while longer. In no time, the release of all the pent-up tension gave me some peace. I fell asleep. An hour later the phone rang. I woke up and stared at the princess phone by the bed. Maybe it was Tim. For a few seconds I considered not answering, but out of curiosity, I grabbed it.

"Mommy, Mommy," Robin said. "I sold more Girl Scout cookies than anyone in the troupe."

I smiled at the sound of her voice. "That's great, honey."

"Are you crying? You sound weird," she said.

I swung my legs over the side of the bed and sat up. "No, I'm okay. Tim left today and it was a little sad. That's all."

Silence. A few seconds passed.

"It means I get to go to camp for free next year. Dad says that's a good thing."

"I'm very proud of you," I said.

"So at Christmas it will just be us?"

I reassured her and tried to change the subject. Anything I could think of: Prince, school, the weather.

"But, Mommy," she said. "We can still see Lynda, can't we?"

I phoned Lynda to tell her about Tim moving out, but she had already heard from him. Suddenly my stoicism faded and I wept again. She allowed me to finish.

"It's better to learn all of your differences now," she said. "And really, Nancy, you're just too much for him now. Probably always."

I grabbed a Kleenex. She'd hit the nail on the head. I wondered, briefly, how she ever accepted it. Maybe someday she'd tell me.

"How about tennis on Saturday morning and then we'll head out to Fiesta Mall and wander?" Lynda said.

I felt better even though I knew she'd beat me to a pulp in tennis. As hard as I tried to trounce her, even with all her suggestions, it never came close to happening. It took me a while to realize that what was important about playing tennis with Lynda wasn't the game at all.

Lynda thought I was funny. She laughed at my jokes and then often tried to tell one herself. They were so bad, or maybe she just told them so poorly, that I had to laugh.

We strolled through the mall looking at all the fall clothes in spite of the Arizona weather—over one hundred degrees in September.

Lynda cleared her throat and locked her arm in mine. "Guy goes into a bar, takes a stool, and orders a beer," she says. "While he waits, he hears a voice say 'That is a great shirt you're wearing.' He looks side to side and turns around. No one is there. His beer arrives and he takes a sip, when he hears a voice, 'You have a fabulous physique.' Again, he looks around and sees nothing.

He finishes his beer and stands to leave, when he hears a voice for the third time: 'You are handsome.' The customer is perplexed and calls the bartender over to explain the mysterious voices. The bartender laughs and explains, 'Oh yeah, I understand. It's the beer nuts ... they're complimentary.'"

I grimaced. Lynda laughed and laughed. "C'mon cookie, that was funny. One of my better ones."

We detoured into a Hallmark store to check out the latest cards—another thing we both liked to do. That day we shared the best ones with each other and didn't buy a thing.

"I'd like to go back to old Scottsdale to a new French restaurant I heard about. I understand they're open for lunch," she said.

As we drove over to the restaurant, I probed to find out what she wasn't telling me.

"Who is the waiter you want to see?" I jabbed her. Lynda often spoke about her fascination with foreign men—the incident with Carlos hadn't been a surprise, and I had agreed on his sexiness—but I did not share her enthusiasm for Frenchmen.

She shook her head. "I've never been to the place. Honest injun. I would admit a devious plan if only I had one."

La Petite Maison had a dozen tables, lots of modern paintings, and flowers everywhere. All the male waiters wore starched white shirts, skinny black ties, and white aprons. They were all French or at least spoke the language fluently. A haughty maitre d escorted us to our table. "Ah mesdames, your waiter will be Jean Claude. He will be with you shortly."

Jean Claude turned out to be over six feet tall, thin, and good-looking once you got past his aquiline, oversized nose. He spoke to us with his head tilted back and never really made eye contact. The arrogance and heavy accent grated on my nerves but Lynda lapped up his attention like a three-year-old. Still, the menu was intriguing and other patrons' dishes made me salivate. All was not lost.

"How old do you think he is?" Linda whispered once Jean Claude disappeared with our orders. I usually had a quick answer for such questions but this guy stumped me. He could be thirty or forty; neither would surprise me. His radar must have alerted him that Lynda was his fan because he visited our table so frequently it became comical, but Lynda hung on his every word.

"Dessert today, ladies?" he said as he cleared our entrees. He eyed Lynda up and down. "You can certainly afford the calories."

I considered throwing up. She smiled with up-tilted eyes and shook her head. "Not today. Maybe some other time."

Some might have said we were stalking Jean Claude as we began to visit La Petite Maison twice a week during that fall. Asking to be seated in his section became a habit. A bad habit, in my opinion, but Lynda was smitten with him. Everything she liked about him went against my taste. I longed to take her back to Tucson and find Carlos.

"Jean Claude is so sophisticated," she swooned one day after he took our order. "You have to give him that, cookie."

"I think he's pretend," I said.

Every laugh line on her pretty face disappeared. "He has manners and style," she said, "and that is something. I certainly wouldn't turn him down."

I choked as I sipped iced tea. "You can't be serious. He's young enough to be your son."

She cocked her head, and instantly I knew what she was thinking. "Okay," I said. "I get it. How can I have any room to talk? But you have to draw the line somewhere, yes?"

"I don't want to date him," she said. "Or get engaged." We both laughed as I felt my neck and face flush. She leaned close as if she were sharing a big secret. "I just want to have a little fun. He could park his shoes under my bed for the night—or maybe the weekend. It's been too long, Nancy."

The early evening call from Lynda inviting me to go with her to Marie Callender's restaurant for pie had to mean something. She usually liked to talk about dessert more than she liked eating it. When she did partake in sweet things, she took baby bites. Her closed eyes would make you suspect she was having an orgasm. In a way, she was.

"Is this a special occasion?" I asked as she peeled out of my driveway and clipped one of the big shrubs.

She smiled and nodded. "Jean Claude was delicious, but I am craving banana crème all of the sudden."

She drove faster than normal. Maybe she had skipped dinner altogether. It was a diet trick she used sometimes.

"You know what?" she said. "I miss my horses. Those were the days, even if those boys twisted my neck and back beyond repair. It was worth it."

Over the ten-year period she spent riding, Lynda had owned six horses, all of them jumpers. When she told me about them, I wasn't a bit surprised to hear that the one she loved the most, Bell O Day, was high-spirited and difficult. It did shock me when she said she enjoyed cleaning the stalls. She claimed the work appealed to her "peasant nature."

"Maybe you should get a horse again," I suggested.

She pulled into Marie Callender's parking lot and drove to the front row. I laughed at her optimism. Sure enough, someone pulled out at the right moment and we parked steps from the front door.

"No more horses, cookie," she said as we got out of the car. "My back will never be the same as it was." She arched her back and rotated her head clockwise and then the opposite way. Her neck cracked several times.

"What exactly is wrong with your back?"

She waved me off. "Nothing. Everything. I fell a lot," she finally said. "They can't fix my spine. All the docs do is prescribe painkillers."

I didn't think any more about it. She complained about aches and pains along with aging in general. Usually she made a joke of it. When I looked at her I saw athleticism, a well-toned body that defied her fifty years, a tanned and youthful appearance. She still played tennis, walked the dog for an hour every day, swam once in a while, and generally did everything I could do. Nothing alarmed me or prompted me to ask more questions.

3

OTHER GUYS

THE JEAN CLAUDE incident awakened desire in Lynda. She began to notice men in a different way. It didn't seem to matter where we were, she criticized the whole package.

"Over there, the guy in the striped shirt. He sells shoes at Penney's," she said. I grinned because it seemed possible. Or another time: "That one, two o'clock. He lives on a cul de sac in Glendale."

She flirted like a twenty-year-old if she liked someone. If it hadn't amused me, I would have been embarrassed.

We sat outside Dairy Queen and licked our cones. Even with all the new ice cream shops everywhere, it was still our favorite. Especially the buster bar, if we felt we could justify the extra calories.

"You know Lynda, we came in different ships but now we're in the same boat," I said. "Both single but wanting a guy."

She smiled. "I don't think so. You are still in Cinderella land and believe you will find a prince, not just a guy. And me? I just want to be serviced. And here's the thing, cookie: I think a prince is still possible for you."

"There were guys after Peter," I said. "Who were they?"

She took one last big bite of her cone and smacked her lips. "Carl, who was married but I didn't know it in the beginning. Billy, ex-football player. Bruce, another beefy ex-football player. I tried on a lot of shoes but there was never a fit. Not really. And truthfully, I didn't want another. For me it was just for fun and trying to forget. Probably."

"Trying to forget about Peter?" I said.

She shook her head violently. "Trying to forget the whole package of what I had with him: hope, something to look forward to every day, and love."

I stared out across the pavement. Her moments of sincerity always came when I least expected them. Maybe I should be her agent, find the right kind of man for her. One who had more to offer than just a roll in the hay. Maybe she picked men who didn't have depth so that she wouldn't have to get involved. It could be a defense mechanism.

"You're still young, attractive, and sharp. There's no reason to give up hope just yet," I said. "I'll start looking around. Let's discuss necessary attributes."

She rested her chin on her hands. "Okay. Nice looking, has a job that he likes and does well at, athletic, not too much into the sauce, six feet tall, has a good disposition, laughs a lot, no baggage, has a full head of hair, plays tennis, and likes cats."

It took a while for the laughter to die down.

"You're so unreasonable," I said. "Men don't like cats."

She nodded. "But if he did, it would show a unique quality that would appeal to me."

"How about a widower who's younger than you?" I said. "Although I have no idea what his position on cats is." She knew instantly that I had someone in mind.

I thought my friend Charlie would be fun, even if he was a little macho. He was successful in business and had a beautiful home. Lynda reluctantly agreed to meet him, and I got right to work on my matchmaking scheme. After not much coaxing, they were eager to meet. Maybe I oversold.

Maybe they expected too much. They had three dates before Charlie asked in disgust, "Are we ever getting to the bedroom, Lynda?"

To my surprise, she went. She said he was bigger than a horse but not as frisky. "It was okay," she said with her eyes down. "I think that dance card has expired though."

Then there was a divorced contractor, a former neighbor, whom I convinced to meet Lynda. Jim liked young ones—they just had to be, at least a year older than his daughter. "A man has principles," he said. I should have known not to shame him into having a date with someone in his decade. It fell flat.

My partner at work, Joe, began fixing me up with blind dates around the same time. Neither my heart nor head were in it. The guys seemed to be cut from the same cloth: jocks, young businessmen trying to make their mark, nice looking, and with a little money to spend. At best it was a distraction.

Another of my friends introduced me to Park, a real estate developer who was converting apartments to condos. He had graduated from Yale and had a pedigree to match. He'd been married once but didn't have children. His background and interests looked good on paper but there was no spark, even though my friend thought he was a catch.

I took Lynda to meet Park for lunch.

On the drive home she confirmed my intuition. "No, you need someone more manly. I hate to say it, but more macho."

Lynda and I limped along like that for several months. Every once in a while, I'd catch a glimpse of Tim at the club. Sometimes he pretended not to see me or he disappeared quickly. I started going at odd times of the day just to avoid seeing him. Eventually, I dropped out of the club altogether and put my house in Tempe up for sale. All of my friends lived and worked in Phoenix, and the commute every day plus trying to meet up with them in the evening took its toll.

The house sold in a week for the full asking price. Lynda congratulated me but was glum the rest of the week. She finally said, "I'll see you less."

I told her that would not happen, but she and I both knew that things would change. And while I continued my search for a soul mate, she had outright stopped looking. She claimed she didn't want or need a man. Whenever I tried to talk with her about it, her caustic humor erupted until she finally said the subject was closed.

"You go on ahead, cookie," she said. "I'll be fine."

One night at 11 p.m., soon after I had settled into my new house in Phoenix, the phone rang, jolting me out of deep sleep. My friends knew that I went to bed at nine. It had to be some sort or emergency or else a wrong number. Semi-awake, I grabbed the phone.

"Please come over right away," Lynda sobbed. "I'm so frightened I don't know what to do."

I rolled off the bed. "What, what is it?"

"Todd called earlier this evening and said he was on his way from California. He needed to talk," she said.

Her raspy voice cracked between sobs. My heart raced as I tried to hold the phone while getting out of my pajamas.

Lynda had heard little from Todd after he moved to California. In the end, he had left Donna behind and ventured out by himself. We hadn't been surprised: Todd had a history of finding fault with his girlfriends. I was amazed that he could even get one, given his short-fused temper and sullen disposition. But as I reminded myself, there is a woman for every guy.

"He got here about thirty minutes ago and started on a rant about what a bad mother I was," she continued. "He raged on and on and then moved toward me with his fist pulled back. I tried to run for my bedroom, but he caught me. He pinned me up against the wall with his arm pressed to my neck," she screamed. "My son!"

"Let's call the police," I said. "Now!"

She moaned. "He's gone, left about fifteen minutes ago. He wanted to kill me, Nancy."

"I'll be right there," I said. For all her tension and fear, I half-expected the house to be in disarray, but when I arrived, there was no evidence of the encounter other than Lynda's disheveled appearance and tear-streaked face. I wrapped an arm around her and led the way to the couch.

She shook some. I stroked her back and held her for a minute. Neither of us spoke.

"You have no idea how much hatred was in his eyes," she said softly. "Complete and total disgust."

I tried to think of something positive to say. Some way to spin what had happened into a simple misunderstanding.

"He let you go," I finally said. "You're safe now."

She nodded. "Only because I yelled at him that I had brought him into the world and I sure as hell could take him out. That did it. He let me go and stormed out of here."

I got up to get her a glass of water. She followed me and apologized for getting me out of bed.

"He will never forgive me for divorcing his father," she said. "That's what this is all about. But it is the last time we'll ever discuss it because I know I'll never see him again."

"Maybe I should make some tea," I said and started to look for teabags and cups.

Lynda took a seat at the kitchen table.

"It's my family's response to illness or any serious problem," I said. "Grandma Lilly's remedy has stuck with all of us."

"I'm just grateful to have you," she said. Then she pointed toward a cabinet and added, "Graham crackers, that'd be good with the tea." She stared out the window even though it was pitch black. I made tea and gave her several minutes of silence. "You know, Nancy, children are over-rated. It's just that simple. I've said it before but if I'd known then what I know now—I'd have had more dogs."

I laughed slightly. It was funny, even if I didn't agree. Lynda's ability to find humor in bad situations was admirable—maybe even her best trait.

Lynda and I shared a love of movies. She humored me on my selections, even though I always picked a chick flick. When *Superman* came out, I was anxious to see it, since it had been my favorite TV serial as a kid. At the last minute, Lynda agreed to join me, but she wasn't keen on it.

We arrived thirty minutes early and were the first to be seated. Lynda enjoyed her popcorn as I relayed all I knew about the making of the movie and the background details of the story.

She smiled and nodded. "I haven't seen you this excited in a long time," she observed. "But actually, this kind of story fits with the whole prince thing."

Finally the lights dimmed, and a mile-long list of credits rolled. "Alright, already," she griped out loud. Several people laughed.

Christopher Reeve hadn't struck me as being right for the part until I saw him on screen. The movie enraptured me and ended too quickly. Lynda got into it after a while but watched quietly.

"Wow," I said. "Looks like there will be a sequel."

She rolled her eyes and linked her arm through mine. "You are too much, cookie. But cute."

We strolled to the car, admired an outstanding vehicle when we saw one, or laughed at a junker. When we got to my Monte Carlo, she pointed to my personalized license plates. Nancee.

"I still can't believe you did that. It seems like such an extravagance for you." I nodded. She wasn't the only one who thought so.

"What's your mother like?" she said as I started the car. "I mean, is she as Mary Poppins as you?"

"Different."

"Tell me about Elise," she said. "And take into account that I still think she is a good mother despite your little chasm. I am in a better position to judge bad mothering having been harassed by a professional—Marie."

"She grew up in a privileged Southern household," I began. "As the youngest, she got more attention and time from her parents. She's sweet, laughs a lot, and is optimistic."

Lynda made a sign for me to continue as I pulled out of the parking lot and headed back to her house.

"She is an attractive redhead. My friends liked her. It's just that she's hard on me. I'm oldest and she expects a lot," I said. "It wears me out."

"I want to meet her," she said like she was ordering at Jack in the Box. "It makes sense. She knows about me and our friendship." I nodded. "And I know about the good and the bad between the two of you. There are no blanks."

Lynda shocked me on a regular basis. I was never prepared for her questions or desires. I teetered from amusement to worry.

"What?" I said. "You're kidding, right?"

"Nope. And I'd like to see Ohio. Never been there. Since you're from there and it sounds like your mother is okay, there must be good stock in Ohio." She stared at me as we walked into her house. "What? Why not?"

"I don't think you two will hit it off at all," I said. "You're so different."

She tossed her purse on the couch and we headed for the beautifully decorated, under-used kitchen.

"Listen, I'm fifteen years older than you," she said. "Your mother is ten years older than me. I am closer to her in age than to you. We probably have more in common than you might think. Let's call her sometime, and I'll decide."

We planned to invite Mom to visit me in Arizona. It was 1979, and by then she had been married to Harlan for twelve years—enough time to discover differences in favorite pastimes. He wasn't much of a traveler, while Mom was always on the go. She especially liked visiting her brother in Florida and her sister in Georgia. Harlan was never comfortable in the upscale Atlanta suburb where Aunt Kitty lived.

"What's Harlan like, compared to your dad?" Lynda said.

That always brought a quandary to the forefront of my mind. Even though Dad had died young and I'd figured Mom would remarry, I never saw what Harlan brought to their union. He was nice enough but bald, short, and stocky. He hadn't been to college, and although I didn't care about that, he seemed defensive. Dad had been tall, vibrant, handsome, but moody. And I was pretty sure, even though I knew Dad hadn't been her first true love, that she had loved him. Mom always noticed powerful and attractive men wherever we were. She commented so often on men who impressed her that I teased her about it. Harlan seemed like the last man she would pick for a husband.

"Maybe Elise was lonely," Lynda said. "Some women need a man around. Or maybe she was scared."

I hated to consider that fear drove her to the first guy she dated after Dad died. Maybe she didn't have the confidence I thought. Or maybe Harlan gave her more compliments than Dad ever had. Maybe he let her be the boss in ways Dad didn't. But none of it had ever been discussed, nor did I think it was any business of mine.

Mom thrilled at the idea to head west alone. I made it out to be a girls' long weekend so Harlan's feelings wouldn't be hurt.

"We'll get some sun, swim, play tennis, and have some fun with Lynda. She's anxious to meet you, Mom." I said. "She thinks you have a lot in common, and I don't just mean red hair."

Mom arrived in early summer. I knew she'd appreciate having something to look forward to after the rigor of another school year. As a teacher, Mom was the primary income earner in the family, while Harlan attempted selling houses. Never was one more ill-suited for sales than he. It used to irritate Mom, but perhaps she had changed.

"Never too late to learn," Lynda said. "Except for me. I don't want to learn another damn thing."

Mom looked all of her sixty years when she got off the plane. The long flight had taken its toll, and I worried, again, if this reunion had been a good idea. I stood apart from the deplaning passengers so I could calm my turbulent stomach.

All the worry faded at the first warm embrace. Mom had tears in her eyes as she stood back from me. "Just let me look at your pretty face. I've missed you these past two years," she said. "You're so thin."

I carried her cosmetic case and she held my hand. As we ambled toward baggage claim, she began to tell me all the news about my brother and sister, whom I talked with periodically.

"Everyone on the plane said it's already over one hundred. Is that true?"

I nodded. "But it's a dry heat. Kind of like a pizza oven." She giggled.

As soon as we retrieved her bag, we headed for the car. When we got outside, she simply nodded like the temperature didn't surprise her. "This isn't so bad. Nothing like the humidity in Ohio."

"I have a big surprise for you once we get home," I said as we turned onto 40th Street. "You won't believe it."

"Can I guess?" she asked. I shook my head. "Oh, I can't wait."

Mom loved Prince. She held him on her lap and oohed over him, then carried him back to the guest room so he could keep her company while she unpacked.

"It is a shock to see you so excited over a cat," Mom said. There had been many cats on the farm but never in the house, and never one as handsome as Prince. And as much as she'd loved cats during my childhood, I had been ambivalent. "What did Robin make of it?"

"She loved him just as much, but she was also perplexed. She said she didn't know I even liked cats."

I fixed her an iced tea as we sat at the kitchen table and caught up on all the Ohio news. She saw Robin on a regular basis as Sam had remained close to her. For the first time, we shared our observations about my daughter without guilt or recrimination. Mom hadn't heard a thing about Sam's new girlfriend and got a kick out of Robin's take on the situation.

"She's so adult. It used to make me so melancholy because she looked so much like you and had so many of your mannerisms, but now I think she's become her own person. The best of both you and Sam," Mom said.

I nodded. Robin would be a force to reckon with in her own way. As frustrating as it could be, I applauded her independence. I hoped she wouldn't have any of my burdens or insecurities.

"Robin couldn't quit talking about Lynda after her last visit," Mom said. "She made an impression."

"They hit it off," I said. "They both have a bit of the ham bone in them—from silliness in all forms to telling jokes. In a way it stunned me. Lynda is not usually a big fan of kids. She even has some mixed feelings about her own."

Mom frowned. "Well, it's not easy being a mother. No one ever tells you exactly what to do. Even with your best efforts you make mistakes. Your kids will remind you."

We cleared the table, and Mom searched around for the cat. Soon she reappeared, cuddling him like precious cargo.

"He's a dear," she said. He purred on command.

We moved into the living room, and I put on a tape of Frank Sinatra that I had bought the week before.

"Sing it to me," she said and sank into the couch. "I didn't know you liked him."

"I've started listening to all of your favorites every once in a while. I'm learning the names of flowers. I stop and talk with strangers in the grocery store ... I think the end is near." We laughed.

"My Way" came on and we both sighed. The lyrics in that song always moved me. Mom seemed affected too, she had such a far-away gaze. After a while, she put the cat down and walked over to an assortment of family pictures on a hall table near the front door: Grandma Lilly and Robin when Robin was three years old, the last picture of Mom and Dad before he died, and a cute one of my brother Rich and me when we were kids. She inspected each one very slowly and then wiped away a tear.

"When will we see Lynda?" she said.

Nothing about the meeting went as I'd predicted. The two women embraced each other spontaneously. There was laughter and affection. Both were anxious to ask questions and learn answers. For a bit, I felt left out of the conversation.

Who could have imagined this?

Lynda lugged out scrapbooks I had never seen. Little did she know that Mom loved photos, not just of her own family. The women went back and forth about the fashions and the places where the pictures had been taken. I finally excused myself to check in with my office. By the time I hung up and returned they were well embedded in Lynda's horse days. There were clippings and articles about some of the shows she had participated in. Many announced awards she'd won and interviews she had given when she was president of the Arizona Exhibitors Association. One front-page newspaper clipping showed Lynda atop Bell O Day, a descendant of Man o' War, as they leaped across a hedge. His beauty matched Lynda's formal riding garb and stately posture. She looked tall. I took a seat and listened to their conversation.

Mom leaned in and turned the page. "This horse dwarfs you," she said with a note of admiration in her voice. "Did you ever fall?"

"All the time," Lynda said. "It's why my back and neck will never be the same. Funny though, whenever it happened, my immediate concern was always for Bell. Sometimes he fell, too. Their legs are so fragile."

"So you've had broken bones?" Mom said. Lynda nodded so vigorously that I wondered if there were more mishaps than she had told me, or perhaps more severe falls than she'd said.

Mom wasted no time getting into Lynda's fabulous pool. She loved swimming and floating around on a raft. Lynda and I sat on the edge and told jokes. The first slightly off-color joke got a reluctant chuckle out of Mom.

"C'mon, Elise. Go ahead and really laugh. That was a good one," Lynda said and Mom obeyed.

Mom swam a few laps. "How many men does it take to change a roll of toilet paper?" she asked.

Lynda shrugged her shoulders.

Mom giggled. "No one knows. Because it's never happened."

I laughed. Lynda laughed bigger. Maybe Lynda was right—Mom was different from what I'd expected. Maybe she had changed. Maybe I didn't know her at all.

Her four-day visit flew by. There were two more afternoons with Lynda and one fabulous dinner at Cork'n Cleaver the night before she left. We talked about men that night.

"There is one thing for sure," Mom said. "I think all women remember the first time they really fell in love."

Mom and Lynda shared a smile.

"That's memory," Lynda said. Still neither looked my way.

Reluctantly I put my hand on Mom's arm. "But it wasn't Dad, right?"

"I loved your dad," she said softly. "But he wasn't my first love. That is something quite different."

I appreciated her honesty but it left me uncomfortable and without a single word to say.

Lynda coughed and picked up her wine glass. "To new friends."

We clinked glasses. Our waitress came by just in time to hear Lynda's toast. "I'll second that one," the girl said.

"Elise, I would love to come visit you in Ohio," Lynda announced. "When is the weather in agreement?"

Mom clapped her hands. "How wonderful. I'd love to have you. August is a good month. We could go into Cleveland and see a play, have lunch at Pier W, go boating on Lake Erie—there's a lot to see and do."

Lynda scrambled to apologize for inviting herself, which only added to the fun of the whole idea. Somehow by then I was confident they'd have a good time, and I wished I could observe the upcoming visit from the sidelines.

Mom and I stayed up late that night. For the first time she wanted to know more about my job. I suspected she had been disappointed to see me leave teaching after five years and had never really understood my fascination with business.

"Business is where the action is," I said. "I like being in the mix that affects our future. There's the politics of it all, not to mention the wheeling and dealing. Then along with the risk, there is more money ... if I make the right decisions."

She smiled, more dutiful than spontaneous. "So you got into business because you could make more money?"

It took some time to explain that more than anything I wanted to be my own boss and be rewarded for success. Success in business equates to money but money didn't drive me. I wanted to build a future that I controlled.

"Selling agrees with my needy personality. Affirmation," I said. Mom seemed lost.

"Most salesmen aren't the social animals that people think. We're actually insecure and like to be alone," I said.

"I didn't know that." She twitched. "Did I do something wrong?"

I faked a yawn, covering my mouth to hide a smile. She often personalized new information that way.

"Absolutely not. It's a part of who I am and how I maneuver through life and work. It's good to know yourself ... what drives and motivates you. I love what I do," I said. "If anything, you helped me, you and Dad. I always believed that I could do whatever I set my mind to do. Perseverance and a plan. Whatever I lack in confidence, I make up for by never giving up. I'm happy to be like that."

We started back toward the bedrooms. She grabbed my hand and squeezed it.

"I'm glad I came. And, I'm proud of you," she said. "And that Lynda is a riot. What a good friend to have. What do you think Vennetta will make of her?"

Vennetta was a teacher friend of hers and also a farmer's wife. Her husband had the Midas touch when it came to money-making schemes. He augmented the income he earned from farming by investing in trucking companies, real estate, and any other opportunity he deemed worthy. He was social and Vennetta was shy, in the same way that Mom was social and Dad had been shy. As different as the two men were, they had seemed to enjoy each other on the rare occasions when our families did things together. Vennetta loved to let others talk and be entertained, so I figured Lynda might just be perfect for her. I knew Lynda would lap up the center-stage status. Harlan was the question in my mind: he was neither social nor attentive, just the kind of bland guy that Lynda sometimes made fun of.

Over the next two months, Lynda shopped and shopped for Ohio outfits, but ultimately she bought only a matching turquoise necklace and bracelet.

"I have nothing to wear on my trip," she said as she stood in the middle of her organized and plentiful closet, which contained enough beautiful clothes to last a decade.

It wasn't that she bought compulsively. Far from it: she paid top dollar for quality and took great care. Then she saved everything, cherishing a memory as much as the item. Despite the lack of purchases on our shopping expeditions, I had learned something in the process.

The new jewelry showcased her red hair to stunning effect. I searched through the racks and pulled out a raw silk pantsuit, a modest bikini and cover-up, some older Bermuda shorts and cotton tops, a light jacket, and she was prepared. "People don't get that dressed up," I said. "Think of the money you saved. You had everything you needed right here."

On the day of the trip, she insisted on being at the airport two hours ahead of time. I was more of the fifteen-minute mindset but didn't argue. The idea that she wanted to go to Ohio still rocked me and I even considered whether she might change her mind.

When I dropped her off at Sky Harbor, we hugged and kissed good-bye. "Have a great time and give everyone my love," I said. I wished I were going with her, but I didn't have any more vacation time left. Men ogled as she snaked through the crowd. She seemed unaware until a handsome older guy smiled at her, and I watched her smile back at him. They exchanged words.

I'll be back Tuesday, big boy. Don't go away. I laughed at my active imagination as I invented what Lynda said. It was probably more like *Hi, how are you?*

Neither Lynda nor my mother phoned from Ohio. For a bit I worried that something might be amiss, but Tuesday came in no time, and I waited at the gate for Lynda's American Airlines flight to arrive. She was almost the first person off the plane and waved when she spotted me.

"Nancy," she shouted. "Ohio will never be the same."

Several people grinned.

"That Cleveland isn't so bad," she added, as she limped her way toward me. "And boy did we have some fun. Sure hope your mama thought so."

"What's with your leg?" I said and pointed.

"Oh nothing," she said. "It's the same old problem with my aching back. Ran out of my happy pills. Lake Erie is big."

I linked my arm through hers and carried her cosmetic case. She leaned on me. I walked at a snail's pace and she hobbled.

When we arrived at baggage claim, Lynda motioned for me to grab her suitcase. As I tried to life it, I almost fell over. She laughed.

"Presents. Lots of presents from Ohio," she said. "We took a boat ride on Lake Erie, she made her famous fried chicken—delicious, I might add. Have you learned the secret?" I shook my head. "We even made it to Higbee's where we had lunch at your favorite, the Silver Grille."

"How was Mom?" I said. She puzzled at my question. "You know, was it easy to be with her?"

"Oh honey, Elise is fine. She worries about all her kids. Even if she doesn't agree with you, it doesn't mean she doesn't love you. She said some things to you that she deeply regrets. I think she learned a lot."

I sighed. "Maybe, but when I left Ohio, it seemed like she was the only one who knew what was best for me."

We strolled toward the parking lot. My mind wandered as I imagined that Robin and I would never have the disagreements I had been through with Mom. I thought myself more modern and with it, more open to divergent opinions and discussion.

"Stop for just a minute," Lynda said. She gripped my arm and her eyes closed.

"What? What is it?" I said.

She winced and dropped her purse. "I need to get home. My back is screaming at me."

As frightened as I'd been by the apparent intensity of Lynda's pain, three days later we were back on the tennis court for our weekly match. I clawed my way through the first two sets, improving but not winning. In the third set, everything clicked. The tennis gods smiled on me, and the game turned in my favor. Of course, they never give it to you easy; you need to muscle forth. A tie-breaker ensued before I claimed victory.

Lynda sashayed to the net and knelt down in mock praise. "Okay, okay. Congratulations, cookie. I knew this day would come."

We laughed our way to the clubhouse and ordered lemonades. I felt like I'd won an Oscar. I danced around the table.

"You are a bad winner," she said. "And I thought the pouts were bad when you lost."

She knew how much I had practiced. There had been many stumbles and spills on the court: I'd missed easy shots, celebrated victory before I had it, made errors on every level. But finally I remembered the lessons and waited for her to tire.

"Winning this tennis match isn't the only reason I feel like celebrating," I said. "I had a mysterious phone call while you were gone."

She scooted her chair closer to me. "Tell me."

The waitress appeared with our lemonades. We gulped the icy drinks. It might have been fall, but hot weather always lingered in Arizona.

"Actually," I told her, "I know him, but not really. Gary lives in Seattle and does the same kind of work I do. He handles big accounts like the navy and the University of Washington. I've seen him at training seminars."

"More, more."

Gary had phoned after Lynda left for Ohio and invited me out to dinner.

"I'm going to visit my favorite uncle somewhere in Mesa in two weeks," he said. "I have a free night and thought it would be fun to get together with you outside business, if you're not attached. Mesa is close to Tempe, right?"

At previous seminars he immersed himself in conversations with other successful salesmen from the West Coast who handled large accounts. He had learned that I didn't have impressive, well-known companies in my territory and the one time he'd chatted with me, he hadn't expressed any special interest in my work experiences or in me as a woman. At least, that had been my take.

We gabbed for a while longer on the phone about work and Arizona. When I mentioned my farm upbringing, Gary teased me, saying that he should take me to meet his Uncle Bernard, a South Dakota crop farmer, since we had so much in common.

"There are different kinds of farms," I said. "We were dairy farmers—the worst of all. Labor intensive, and the cows must be milked twice a day. Your uncle has crops. They don't need daily attention. Plus you said he has ten thousand acres, and we had 126. Not the same."

Uncle Bernard sounded more successful than Dad had been—Bernard's farm supported three families and had quite a long history. Like many Midwest farmers, though, he sounded like a down-to-earth guy with a love of animals, respect for nature, and devotion to his family. No matter how much success he'd had, nothing had changed him. I told Gary I wished I could meet him; he sounded like my kind of guy.

Then, out of the blue, Gary asked about my dad. There was no way for him to know that I still hated talking about his death twelve years earlier, at the age of forty-eight. Gary immediately got that it was a sensitive subject and gave me time to compose myself.

"I was only twenty when he died. He was the leader of the pack," I said, in hopes that my joke would help me out of a sinking feeling.

He listened. I talked more. And then some more. Afterwards, I exhaled and felt better. As relieved as I was, it had been a one-sided conversation. Who'd have predicted I'd commit my own biggest pet peeve?

"My dad died when I was nineteen, eight years ago," Gary said. "No one understands how much it still bothers me, except maybe now you. Even Mom has adjusted."

"Where are you in the pecking order?" I said.

When he told me the middle of five, I almost choked. The forgotten child. I wanted to tell him that explained why his father's death was so hard. But before I could decide how to phrase it, he surprised me.

"I was Dad's favorite, and not just because I looked like him," he said tenderly. "When I was little, I crawled into his lap every day when he came home from work. I'd kiss and hug him. He called me his little lover boy."

Tears formed in my eyes. How much I had wanted affection from my father, and how infrequently I'd received it. I couldn't remember many kisses other than the ones I'd gotten after he spanked me. I relayed to Gary how Dad kissed us after punishment and made us kiss him back.

"That makes perfect sense," Gary said. "He wanted you to know that it was your action that got the spanking, but he still loved you. I never got spanked. Instead we got lectures that lasted an hour. I'd rather have had the spanking."

We laughed. I glanced at the clock. We had talked for thirty minutes long distance.

The attention flattered me. I remembered thinking how cute he was the first time I saw him. I also liked his accomplishments and how understated his ego seemed, considering his success—it was a dichotomy I admired. I found myself excited and eager for the upcoming dinner.

When I summed up the phone call to Lynda with "he's not your average white boy," she howled.

Then she reminded me that she had veto power.

The week zoomed by. On the night of the dinner, I changed my clothes three times. I opted for middle-of-the-road: pants and a v-neck sweater. I brushed out my shoulder-length hair as straight as I could muster and paced in the living room. A few butterflies.

When he pulled into the driveway and walked to the front door, he spotted me through the large picture window and waved. *Shorter than I remembered.* I liked his too-long hair, though. It screamed unconventional. His faded jeans and "members only" jacket were quite a departure from the fancy suits I'd seen him wear in the seminars.

Prince leaped from his perch atop the couch and hurried to the front door.

"Wow, big cat," Gary said as he leaned down to give him a scratch. "You look nice, Nancy. Good to see you." He offered a handshake. I took his hand in both of mine, slightly confused.

"I thought we'd go to Garcia's in Scottsdale," he said. "I love Mexican food, and they say it's famous. The best."

It was a bit of a trek, but I didn't want to discourage him. The restaurant had quite a following in several locations but the original restaurant in Scottsdale was considered by many to be their flagship. In any case, Gary and I would have more time to get to know each other.

"This is some weather, September and still a hundred. Guess I won't need my jacket," he laughed.

"Maybe in December you'd need it," I said. "Well, only in the morning."

"So a raincoat probably isn't something you own either?"

I shook my head. "Or an umbrella. Both of which are probably every-day necessities in Seattle. I was only there once, when I was sixteen. It rained both days."

As we drove north on Scottsdale Road toward the restaurant, we passed a portion of the ASU campus, apartment complexes, and occasionally an undeveloped lot. There were mesquite and palo verde trees, flowering shrubs, but not much grass and the terrain was flat. He seemed to be taking it all in.

"This is so different from the northwest," he said. "What is it about the cactus everywhere?"

"It is the desert, you know. We need a place for the rattlesnakes to hide."

His head jerked around until he saw my grin.

There was a wait at the restaurant. We sat on the patio among glowing torches and strolling mariachis. We munched on chips and salsa and sipped gigantic margaritas while we waited for a table.

"I could go for this year round," he said.

"You might not think so in July or August," I said. "In those months we fry eggs on the sidewalk."

For just a second he believed me. Or so I thought.

"You can't get me twice," he said and poked me.

After dinner we strolled around old Scottsdale and window-shopped in front of art galleries and jewelry stores.

"Lots of horses and cowboys," he joked. "And don't forget the silver."

"You've got it pegged. Still, I like to look," I said. "They say shopping is about education, not buying."

"I like that, but the American retailers probably wouldn't," he said. "Saving is more important to me than anything."

I nodded but his remark stunned me. He dressed in trendy suits with all of the right accessories. I had misjudged him—and happily so.

.

"This was fun," he said when we got to my house. "Maybe we can do it again some time."

A sweet, light kiss at the door ended the night. It had been a good date without any awkwardness or uncomfortable moments. He was easy to be with. I had no idea where the whole thing could lead—he lived in Seattle and I was in Phoenix: a tough dating scenario.

Over the following weeks, Lynda and I discussed each of Gary's attributes in minute detail. I always came back to the geography problem. She said I could overcome such a puny issue.

Gary called once in a while. Not as often as I thought he would, given how well the date went, but I didn't know what to expect. Maybe it felt like foreign territory to him as well.

A couple of months later I learned just how serious the back and neck pain was for Lynda. She called one Friday afternoon and asked if I could be so kind as to drive her to the doctor's office. She never had much respect for doctors, always saying the fact that they "practiced" medicine should be your first clue about their ability to treat your ailments. But on the phone that afternoon, she spoke in sentence fragments amid groans. I hurried to her house and helped her into the car, arranging several pillows around her to ease her discomfort.

Several hours later, we walked out of Dr. Chandler's office. He talked with me before we left.

"She needs rest," he said in a staid doctor sort of way. "And no physical activity for at least a week. I've told her that she needs to make changes in her life, but I have a feeling she ignores me."

Changes? But she never rests.

She leaned on me as we headed to the car. Nothing suited her. Her entire demeanor had transformed.

"Are you okay?" I said.

"I needed the shot," she said. "They just don't last as long as they used to. And I ran out of the Feldene."

"What shot?"

"Cortisone," she said. "It's all bad news."

She slumped in the seat. Her chin rested on her chest. She was so depressed, broken in a way. Once we got on the freeway, I reached over and gripped her hand. It was cool and limp.

"Doctors can fix anything now," I said. She didn't look up. Her eyes stayed closed. I patted her hand, "You'll get better."

Lynda groaned. "You don't understand. My back and neck are twisted beyond corkscrew. Now I have arthritis in my hip. Even if he fixes it with a replacement, there is no solution for the rest. He doesn't want me to play tennis or even walk. What kind of a life would that be?"

The seriousness of Lynda's words when she'd gotten off the plane from Ohio hadn't registered. She could be dramatic and overplay both positive and negative emotions. I often had backaches after a long airplane flight, and I'd assumed this incident was just that—a single occurrence. Pain could scare anyone. Now, I drove faster than usual.

It took strength to get her out of her clothes and into bed. The tightness in her face was gone, but her eyes glazed over.

"I've been worried about this for a while," she said. "The doctor's warning today wasn't the first time." I frowned.

She rubbed her temples and pulled the covers up around her body despite the hum of the air-conditioning. I considered returning to the doctor's office without telling her, to ask for more information.

"The doc said that being active would hasten the onset of more serious problems," she said. "And in order to be active, I needed the drug. It's a double-edged sword."

"Is Feldene a narcotic?" I asked. She nodded.

I held her hand. We didn't talk for several minutes.

"Does Tim know about this?" I asked.

"He knows about the injuries and the cortisone shots," she said. "But I have never discussed my health with the kids."

"I could go to Dr. Chandler's office and speak with him about the options going forward," I said.

She shook her head. "Need to sleep, cookie. Can you put the dirty clothes in the washer before you go? We'll talk about this later."

It was after 4 p.m., too late to go back to work. Plus the whole scene had traumatized me. My invincible role model had dimmed. If this could happen to her, could it happen to me?

Two days elapsed before Lynda felt like having company. She opened the front door and then staggered across the living room behind me. I would be making dinner.

"You're much better," I said, even though I didn't think so.

She shot me a dirty look. "You are such a bullshitter. Cute though, and thoughtful. What are you serving tonight?"

"First wine, and then I'll give you choices," I said.

She grinned. "Wine sounds good. In fact, the whole bottle."

I uncorked the bottle she pointed to and let the wine breathe. She said it tasted better that way and it was the proper thing to do. Maybe true, but I was always in a hurry to have the first sip.

"So really? No more tennis? I could beat you every time," I teased.

She wagged her finger at me. "Have you no shame? You're such a bad girl. I need to talk with your mother."

"You already did. Plus, I'm sure she told you that she couldn't do anything with my behavior either." I placed the generously filled wine goblet in front of her. I pulled steaks out of the refrigerator and seasoned them while she offered advice. I ignored her and proceeded to cut up veggies for the salad. A baked potato sounded good, but I knew from experience she'd object. "Have to save calories for the ice cream or pie," she often said.

"Seriously, what exactly did Dr. Chandler say?" I said.

"I could have hip replacement, but that wouldn't solve a thing with the back and neck," she said. "The hip deal would cost about $30,000 or so. Chandler would refer me to an orthopedic surgeon."

"Insurance would cover it though, yes?" I said.

She shook her head. "Not in my case."

I grabbed my wine and sat down beside her. "Why?"

"So many things were excluded as prior conditions, I got mad and cancelled my insurance last year. Although the hip probably would have been covered," she admitted.

"And the drug, Feldene?" I said.

She fidgeted in her chair. "Six years is a long time to be on something so strong. There isn't much benefit from it anymore."

We sat without making eye contact. There had to be something she could do to get better and reclaim her life. Idle didn't fit.

"If you had the hip surgery and didn't play tennis, you could probably walk. That would be okay," I said. "Walking is great exercise, without the strain on the body."

She reached out and touched my arm. "I appreciate your concern. It is hard for you to understand the place I'm in right now, and I don't want you to be frightened. Long ago, I knew the consequences of my choices."

Years before I met Lynda she divested her stock portfolio into bonds, some stocks, and moved a large portion of cash into a Mexican bank that paid 10 percent interest per year. She claimed it was completely safe. The decision was met with great resistance from Mr. Shapiro, her soon-to-be retired financial advisor. She loved and hated the guy. I am sure Lynda had something to do with his early retirement decision, since I heard the stories of their ongoing debates over the best and safest investments. Lynda liked to take a different road even though she claimed to be risk-adverse. When I teased her about the similarity between her financial decisions and Tim's, she jumped on me.

"No way. Not at all the same. My money is still there—it's in Mexico and I can get to it whenever I want. When it grows to two million pesos, I'll take it all out," she said. "Tim's money is gone. That was a pipe dream."

"How do you get it out? Do you have to go in person?" I said.

She scrunched up her face. "Of course I just phone them. I talk to the manager and give him my account number and so on. Not any different from here."

"I'd say it's different from here. Mexico has a reputation for taking property, so how do you know that bank wouldn't confiscate your money?" I said. "And how did you ever find the bank in the first place?"

And exactly how much is a "large portion" of money? As many times as I heard the details, I had never asked and she'd never offered. Really, it was none of my business.

Lynda changed the subject to my dating life. As much as I liked Gary, the whole long distance thing continued to plague me. I had decided not to count on it, going forward. That week I was scheduled to have lunch with a friend of one of my customers. My blind date, Phil, was an accomplished contractor, divorced, and raising two teenagers.

I had never been interested in older men, or even men my own age. Somehow, ever since high school, when I'd developed a crush on a sophomore during my senior year, I'd dated younger men, and I never looked back. The possibility of suddenly going the other way intrigued me. At least the guy probably wouldn't be intimidated by a successful working woman. Plus, I had a child to raise, myself, even if only part-time, so we would have that in common. Lynda and I agreed it was worth further exploration. I laughed when she urged me to find out his company's address and scope him out ahead of time.

Why I worried about age any longer I have no idea. Phil turned out to be tall, in fairly decent shape, a good dresser and secure in how he handled himself. He was the type of guy you might see and admire once but not do a double take. However, once you talked with him, his attractiveness quotient moved up several notches. He listened when I talked and laughed at my quirky observations about working with so many men—both in the office and as customers. Lunch passed in record time and I accepted a dinner date.

"How old is he?" Lynda asked that evening.

I had been distracted during the lunch date trying to figure out that very thing. Starting with his children's ages and doing the math, I suspected he had to be forty or so. Certainly, by comparison to Tim, it would be a quantum leap for me. Picturing the two men side by side made me smile.

"I like him," I said. "He's just a regular guy: hard-working and nice. I need more info."

"Not so fast, cookie. It'll take a lot to impress me," she said.

Phil and I dated for a month. I met his children (Jake and Anna) who were cordial and inquisitive. Their interest surprised and charmed me. They asked about Robin, my work, and what sports I liked. We had some humorous exchanges about their dad's wardrobe choices. They hoped I would update his fashion sense.

Robin made a quick visit to Phoenix in February, and I jumped at the chance to have her meet the new guy. Maybe even have her meet his teenagers. She seemed interested, which encouraged me.

The kids were twice Robin's age, but she handled herself like a pro. Phil picked out some fancy-schmanzy French restaurant, which I questioned but he insisted was one of the best. When we arrived, many of the staff took a minute to say hello to Phil and the kids. Robin wasted no time eying the décor and studying the menu.

"Mom, there's nothing less than thirty bucks on this menu," she said, a little too loud.

We all laughed. Phil intervened.

"Robin, don't you worry. Order anything at all you want. This is my treat," he said.

Robin shrugged. "Okay, if you say so."

I wondered just how far she'd go with such encouragement. She seemed to have developed quite the Midwest appetite—large portions. That night I discovered that while she might have been from Ohio, the kid had learned something about fine dining from her grandparents. Somewhere she had developed a taste for filet mignon and lobster.

Everyone got a chance to talk that night. We shared stories and even told jokes. There were no awkward moments or lapsed silences. I watched Robin give each person the once-over.

What makes an impression when you're a kid?

We got home by nine. I waited for Robin to say what she thought. We played with Prince in the living room. She rifled through the hall table drawer for checkers and then set up the board.

"Dad has been helping me. I don't think you can beat me anymore," she said with a big grin.

"What did you think about Phil?" I finally said.

She laid all the checkers out on each side without glancing up. Prince stayed by her and she petted him from time to time. At first I wondered if she had heard my question because she took so long to answer.

"He's okay," she said. "But, he's too old for you. What do you want, red or black?"

Finally a mature, financially and emotionally stable guy had entered my life, the kind of guy I wanted to like—maybe even fall in love with—and she'd nixed it. I was irritated but not surprised. She had the veto power that Lynda claimed.

I sighed and pointed to red.

Shortly after Robin returned to Ohio, her doubts proved right. Phil confessed that he was in love with another woman who would not be a good match for him.

"I know it would be a disaster and I'm trying to move on. But I'm not ready yet," he said. "Maybe you can wait for me?"

We parted friends. Mostly.

"Time to start over," Lynda said. "Just as well. You know, kids are very perceptive. Especially that little cookie of yours."

Work improved. My sales increased in direct proportion to the amount of effort I put forth. The extra cash made me feel better about myself and gave me a sense of security. I began to save. Lynda wanted me to invest, but I liked the idea of watching my savings account accumulate. To me, that was the place to start.

"I'm almost there," she said one day. "The two million pesos. And then what to do, that is the question."

"Do you want to spend it, invest it, or what?" I asked. She shrugged; then smiled. I poked her. "I'd love to have that dilemma."

Whenever we discussed money, we seemed to become oblivious to all else. We concentrated on the questions and debated our opinions. Such was the case that day as the gardener busied himself trimming weeds and bushes. Distracted with our usual banter about, we didn't realize Ralph had been outside until maybe an hour had passed. He usually stayed close to the back door, but now he was nowhere to be found. When we got to the front gate, we noticed it was open.

At first we scrambled around the front of the house and the immediate neighborhood. Then we got in my car and drove down every street, stopping anyone we saw to ask if they'd seen a black cocker spaniel. Nothing turned up.

Two days later, Lynda got a call from someone who'd seen Ralph's body beside the road three miles away. I went with her to retrieve him. The sight nearly undid me. "My first childhood dog, Nelly, was hit by a car and didn't die right away. We watched her suffer," I said to Lynda as wrapped him up in burlap. She insisted on burying him at her house.

There were many tears. She berated the gardener for his carelessness. He broke down and cried. She wilted then, and ended up consoling him. He offered to buy her another dog, give her free landscaping, anything to assuage his guilt.

"Javier, these things happen," she said. "Your apology is enough. Just be careful from now on. I'll get another dog."

I was proud of her. Maybe a little surprised, but amazed at her conciliatory attitude. I wondered, though, about her mention of another dog. Poor neurotic little Ralph had appealed to her.

Nevertheless, a week later she called to invite me to meet George, a rescued German shepherd. "He's five years old, neutered, and trained," she said. "I decided I might as well have a guard dog."

George was a big boy with an oversized head. He made a formidable statement with his bark that came from a deep place. What I quickly learned was the bark wasn't a warning of more aggressive behavior; it was the end of the story. After barking, he usually moved on to lie down on the kitchen floor.

He obeyed commands and watched every move Lynda made. I put my hand down and motioned for him to come, and he obeyed. I petted his head and scratched his ears.

"Was George his name?" I said.

Lynda shook her head. She spelled out Bo. "What a stupid name. You can rename any pet in a few days by just repeating the new name. Look at him. He's as comfortable as an old shoe. George."

He moved over to her outstretched hand and nuzzled into it. Lynda bent down and kissed the top of his head. Then she moaned and rubbed her back.

"It's just you and me, big boy," she said to the dog. "How about a biscuit?" His tail thumped against the floor. Obviously he had already learned that word.

"How is your back?" I asked her.

She twitched. "Dr. Chandler is referring me to Dr. Russo about the hip thing. He wants to confirm that it is the hip that's my main problem and not my knee. God, my whole body is shutting down. Then there's all that money for the replacement, and I'd still have the back problem. That's much worse. How will I ever have fun again?"

"But not fixing the hip will put more strain on the back, no?" I said.

She let George out on the patio and watched him for a bit. "He's a smart one, don't you think?"

"Lynda, let's be positive about the future. You can get better," I said. "Fix the hip and try a different medication for the back and neck."

She swallowed. "It's hard to explain how I feel. My body not cooperating. How helpless and defeated. Never without pain. I doubt you've ever been in such a state. And I hope you never are."

I moved to the cupboard to look for teabags and cups. She smiled and nodded.

"Grandma Lilly and the tea again," she said. "I'm desperate. I'll try anything, cookie."

I didn't know what to say.

Gary phoned to find out whether I planned to attend a training seminar Xerox was holding in Los Angeles. I told him I did. We didn't know it at the time, but the meeting was scheduled for the same weekend as the NCAA final championship. March, 1979: Larry Bird vs. Magic Johnson. There would never be a showdown like this again, was the recurring theme in every newspaper.

Apparently Xerox's events planner was not much of a sports fan. The twenty-eight men who showed up for the seminar couldn't believe we were scheduled for a cruise on Newport Yacht Basin that night.

"Is there a TV on the boat?" they asked.

An enormous yacht arrived at the dock; someone said it was over a hundred feet long. The guys rushed aboard to find the TV that was reported to be set up in the living room. Gary hung back and strolled up the ramp with me. He had saved a spot for me that morning at the training session, which had caused a few guys to raise their eyebrows. It surprised me as well. Sitting next to him made it hard to concentrate on the material. I wanted to look him over and ask ten thousand questions. The presenter spoke in a monotone, there weren't many breaks, and the chairs were stiff.

"Is this game important to you?" I asked him now. He shrugged.

"I can see a basketball game any time," he said. "But you live in Phoenix, and I'm in Seattle. It's not every day a guy gets a chance to cruise Newport in style with a beautiful woman."

Our easy conversation extended throughout the night, amid all the yelps and whistles over the basketball game emerging from inside the ship. Gary and I were the only people outside, other than the bartender.

The warm springtime air and marine smells intoxicated me. He asked about Robin and her father, how long we were married, why we divorced. When I told him the marriage had lasted four years, he nodded and said that his had been about the same.

"We divorced because she wanted kids and I didn't," he said without emotion. "Actually, I said we were too young, but no matter. It ended without bitterness. She married someone else almost immediately and got pregnant."

"And I had a child because Sam begged me," I said. "Not that I regret it, but I wasn't the driving force."

"What does Robin want to do when she grows up?" he asked. "Or is nine too soon to have such plans?"

A few men showed up on deck during halftime, but their sole interest was the game between Indiana State and Michigan State. Everyone talked over each other, predicting how it would end. It made me want to watch the second half even though I didn't follow college basketball. All bets were off when people said things like the best game ever, two greats like this would never be seen again, years from now we'll all remember where we were on this night, and what will happen when these two reach the pros?

In no time the deck emptied out. Gary and I were left alone again. The slight breeze increased and the yacht rocked some. My stomach lurched. As much as I wanted to concentrate on what Gary was saying, I used all my powers to keep from getting sick. All I could think about was how much I wanted land. And a bed. And a toilet.

What a way to make an impression.

Lynda chuckled at my dramatized version of the yacht adventure. She said I should phone Gary if my stomach ever righted itself. I wasn't sure he had much interest in me after sacrificing the game of the decade to nurse a seasick chick. The experience had been humiliating.

Once more I turned my attention to work and making money. Plus I'd have Robin for the summer in three months, and I needed to plan for day camp or other activities while I worked. She had a history of raising a fuss when it came to meeting new kids. Once I got her to camp though, she adapted and drank in the fun. Words like "they don't have anything like this in Ohio" were common. I made a practice of getting to work early and hitting it hard for six hours or so, to be done by mid-afternoon. Then we'd head for the swimming pool at my condo and usually have it all to ourselves.

Gary called occasionally, but I couldn't read his interest level or intentions. He asked me questions about Robin—how she survived our wretched heat and if she ever got homesick. It touched me. In a way, his concern made me wonder if he regretted his decision not to have children when he was married to Laurie. Finally, I asked him. He hesitated before answering.

"If I could have a kid who started at age ten, I'd sign up tomorrow. The baby phase is just not my thing, but you know, you have to go through it. I'm pretty sure I'd be exhausted by the time I got to my favorite part," he said. I empathized with him. Robin's baby years had not been my favorite part, either. The older she got, the better job I did as a mother.

Gary and I talked about sales ideas and our customers. He listened more than any other salesman I'd ever been around. I complimented him on it.

He laughed. "You can't learn anything about a customer or anyone else if you're talking."

Interesting. How true.

Summer blasted its way into Arizona and set up camp for what everyone knew would be three brutal months. Robin and I swam and melted our way through the first month and then Gary surprised us with a visit. He claimed he had some business in town, though he never disclosed exactly what it was. The hotel he picked was close to my condo. I was relieved I didn't have to worry about a potentially awkward sleeping arrangement.

As tough a critic as Robin had been about my prior boyfriends, she and Gary clicked from the first afternoon.

"Gary, do you know Marco Polo?" she yelled to him just before she splashed into the pool.

He wasted no time diving in and coming up near her. "Come'n get me," he said, then slipped below the surface and emerged on the other end of the pool.

Her eyes were squeezed shut. She smiled. "Marco?" she called out.

"Polo!" Gary called. Robin laughed loud and long. As she approached him, he got out of the pool and tiptoed back to the opposite side. It took her a while to catch on to his devious tactic.

"Gar, that's cheating!" she yelled when she finally caught him.

"Just bending the rules," he shrugged. "Marco never said anything about staying in the water the whole time."

When they tired of the game, they competed to see who could make the biggest cannonball. Gary showed off with a back flip before one of his splashes. She retaliated with a splayed maneuver that soaked me and left her with a sore belly.

"I think you beat me fair and square," Gary conceded after at least a dozen attempts.

Robin grinned. "Me-thinks so too!"

On Gary's second night I decided to have a barbeque and invite one of my best friends, Ann, and her boyfriend. We planned to have burgers, cole slaw, and chips. Robin instructed Gary on how to work the gas grill, since she had watched me use it before. Flames shot up as he dropped the patties on the grill, but he forgot to turn down the heat.

We all gathered around the dinner table and took bites. Robin eyed Gary and then her burger. "Gar," she said, "these burgers are burnt to a crisp. And you tried to fool us by covering them with cheese."

"Out of the mouths of babes," Gary said sheepishly.

The honesty of their beginning predicted the future. They connected and discovered how much they liked to tease and be teased.

That week, Gary treated us to miniature golf, go-kart racing, and our favorite, Dairy Queen. He knew how to impress a kid. And me. Everything about the three of us together was easy. Not only did Gary's visit end too soon, Robin moped around afterwards.

"It's not as much fun without Gary," she said. Then she asked, "You like him too, don't you?"

A week after Gary and Robin had left Arizona, I got back into daily contact with Lynda, who was still struggling. She said the pain and discomfort had worsened. She called me the night before her appointment with Dr. Russo and asked if by chance I'd be able to go with her to the office. I assured her I would, my plans could always be altered.

She sat quietly in the passenger seat and stared straight ahead. I respected her desire not to talk and tuned into her favorite radio station, KUPD. Crazy Dave's antics always amused her. This time, she didn't react at all. A sour expression aged her, and hunched-over posture didn't help.

"Tell me what's going in your life," she said, finally.

I considered. Things were good with Mom and Robin. There was money in my checking account. My body was cooperating with running and exercise. My relationship with Gary was moving forward. It didn't feel right to talk about any of it. Especially to Lynda. As much as she'd had the world by the tail when I met her, she had fallen behind.

"The next song goes out to my momma on her birthday," Crazy Dave said on the radio. Frank Sinatra's "I'll Be Seeing You" began to play.

Tears followed each other silently down Lynda's cheeks. She always said how much she hated to cry, how it embarrassed her. Now she struggled to regain composure. "Peter ... he used to sing that song to me. Rather, he tried to sing it. I don't know why ... the words didn't make sense then." I quickly changed the channel but she turned it back. Her gaze drifted out the window. Neither of us spoke.

Walking the short distance from the car to Dr. Russo's office zapped her strength.

The waiting room was jammed with patients in various stages of debilitation. Some had canes, some were in wheelchairs. Lynda leaned on me until I spotted two seats together. She grumbled something as I steered her toward a chair.

We'd arrived on time but the delay to see Dr. Russo was nothing short of agonizing. Lynda hated to wait for anything. She looked at her watch every couple of minutes and sighed. It took all my cunning and imagination to hide my own aggravation and keep her under control.

I knew from experience that if I didn't, she would be a bear to the doctor.

"Want a magazine?" I said. She shook her head and crossed her arms over her chest.

"I want a life," she said, barely audible.

The woman sitting in the adjacent seat tapped her arm and smiled. "Me too. What are you here for?"

The woman wore a stylish jogging suit. Her gray hair was pulled back in a chignon, and her skin was nearly flawless. She was so attractive, I looked twice. She could have been an old movie star. Lynda perked up. She enjoyed beautiful people of any age.

"I'm here to see if this guy can fix my gnarled hip," she said.

The woman nodded. "I had it done six months ago. Best decision I ever made. And it wasn't that painful. You know, compared to child birth." She smiled. "Dr. Russo is the best."

Lynda scowled. "They all say that about themselves. Men. But I appreciate your recommendation. The last several months have been bleak."

A nurse appeared and called the woman's name. She wished Lynda well and walked away. Lynda focused on every step. I did the same.

"She's moving okay, don't you think?" Lynda said.

I grabbed the comics section of a newspaper that someone had left and turned to the puzzles. "C'mon, help me on this," I said. "It could be a while."

She grumbled some more but put on her glasses and studied. "One down is dose. Ha, that's funny," she said.

"Maybe we should read your horoscope, give you something else to concentrate on," I said.

Over an hour later, Lynda emerged from the doctor's office. My heart sank when I saw her. She'd been crying, and her hair stuck out all over. She stopped to settle her bill without saying a word. I tried to help her to the door, but she pushed my arm away. We walked the short distance to the car without speaking.

"He can't do a thing, cookie," she said, once I started the car. "This is black Monday."

I drove toward the freeway and shook my head. "So, we try another doctor. I just can't accept that."

"There's too much damage ... back, neck, and hip. I'm a wreck. Not much surprise there. Not really," she said. "He recommends drugs to deal with it. He must not have read Chandler's notes too well. I have already drugged my body to death."

We rode in silence.

"I need a nap," she finally said. "A really, really long nap."

She closed her eyes. Even a suggestion about pie at Marie Callender's got no reaction. For a second I assumed she hadn't heard me. I started to repeat the question, but she stopped me.

"I need to clear my head. Figure out how in the hell I am going to manage with all these changes. And disability," she said.

My face flushed. I'd made light of a serious predicament, but all I'd meant to do was think of something that would make her feel better. Pie had always worked wonders for her.

Traffic was light for midday. When we got to her house she insisted on getting herself inside. "I know what to do," she said. "Give me a few days, though."

I began running twice as much, to kill time. My appointment book jammed with demonstrations and cold-calls. At home, I worked on the house like it was a spring cleaning project. I gave Prince his first bath, much to his objection. Anything to keep busy. Anything to keep my mind off Lynda's health. I jumped every time the phone rang, thinking it was her. But no, it was a running buddy, a friend from work scheduling a get-together for someone's birthday, a wrong number. Nights were restless. Vivid and dark dreams remained fresh in my mind when I awoke. I wanted to solve her problem but I couldn't.

"A few days" is three, right? Should I wait four?

I called Mom. It hadn't been in my plan. But one day I picked up the phone and dialed. She listened. I cried some.

"There must be something I haven't thought of," I said. "She was so healthy."

Mom cleared her throat. "We talked about the pain when she was in Ohio. I noticed her limping one morning. At first she made a joke about it, but I could tell she was worried."

"But she played tennis, walked, and never had a problem before," I said refusing to accept recent events, as if that would change the situation.

"She hid it from you. I suppose she must have hid it from you," Mom said.

I wanted to scream. It had been a mistake to call her. She didn't have any ideas on what else I could do. No words of wisdom like I remembered from my childhood. Not even encouragement.

"Nancy, there are times when doctors don't have a remedy because there is none. Remember what happened with your dad?" she said.

Dad had a brutal heart attack at forty-eight. There was no way to repair the scar tissue that surrounded his heart. Several years later, Mom told me that the best cardiologist at the Cleveland Clinic had told Dad, half-jokingly, that the only solution would be a new heart. The doctor told him to get his affairs in order because he probably only had two years to live. That prediction proved accurate. I slouched in my chair and twisted the phone cord around my finger. It had been twelve years since that horror show.

"How did you deal with it, Mom?" I asked. "It could have happened at anytime, anywhere."

She gave a bewildered sigh. "I really don't know. We both wanted to enjoy the remaining time. Not be fixated on death. It's amazing what the human mind can endure, overcome."

"And none of us kids knew a thing. We thought Dad would get better," I said.

Mom had proved to be stronger than Dad. She acted like she always had—she giggled a lot, got upset if we didn't do our homework or if Dad decided he didn't want to go to church, took the teasing we gave her if the biscuits she made were hard as rocks. Dad went into a funk a month after he got home from the hospital and never regained his composure.

He hardly ever smiled, never laughed, wasn't interested in our school stuff, didn't care if we didn't do our homework or brought home an unimpressive report card. All because he knew his time was short.

"Did Lynda seem depressed to you, when you saw her?" I asked. Maybe I had approached her problem from a physical perspective, when I should have been thinking about the emotional side of the issue.

"She makes a joke about everything. I guess if you analyzed her personality, there is tragedy. But that's how life is," Mom said. "She seems to be so realistic about life, almost without emotion. I think that's unusual."

Moving to the condo had freed up the time I used to spend on outdoor chores and put me half an hour closer to work, but now Lynda lived thirty minutes from me. We rarely met up for the spontaneous dinners or late-night ice cream dashes that had been frequent when I lived in Tempe. I felt as if I had abandoned her even though she never said a word about it. In fact, she'd encouraged the move, citing how much easier life would be for me.

"We'll figure it out," she'd said on the day I moved. "You aren't getting out of my life, cookie."

I thought I saw a tear, but maybe not. Guilt plagued me as I held the picture in my mind.

4

EVERYONE MOVES

GARY CALLED MORE often. We talked longer. Soon he began to call every day. Then sometimes he phoned again at night, before bed. I shared some of the guilt I harbored over my move into Phoenix, away from Tempe and Lynda.

"How did you meet her again? Or didn't you ever tell me?" he asked one night. I hesitated and then relayed how my relationship with Lynda had begun with Tim.

He laughed. "I'd say you've grown up since then. I'm only six years younger than you. Am I too old?"

That wasn't funny. The guys at work still ragged on me occasionally, too. I pleaded with them that there should be a statute of limitations on idiot behavior, but any comment I made only added fuel. Joe, my partner, told me privately it could take a while for the fun they had to die down.

"When do I get to meet Lynda?" Gary asked.

"Well, Gary," I over-explained," You do live fifteen hundred miles away, so it might not be too easy for her to drop by. Anyway, she probably wouldn't be excited about the rain."

"Good point. In fact, I'm tired of waiting for sunshine, and cold has arrived in Seattle. How about I come to meet her in a couple of weeks?"

I hung up on an air of optimism.

Lynda had eventually called me about a week after that terrible doctor appointment, but her situation hadn't really improved. She continued her downward health spiral, but she never gave me any details other than "pain, more pain." When I asked, she usually changed the subject to ask about my business or progress with Gary. As much as I believed I had learned about him, she'd always come up with something I hadn't thought of, like what were his siblings' personalities compared to his, was he still close to his mother, did he ever consider moving from Seattle.

"I wish you had a photo," she said one day at lunch. "How tall is he? You know how you like to wear those high heels."

Gary was 5'9", shorter than any guy I'd been with. He had an athletic body, a cute smile, and hazel eyes, and with his sleepy eyelids, long hair, and thick lips, he looked somewhat like Mick Jagger. I found a picture of the rocker and showed it to Lynda.

"Kind of like Mick. That's what Gary looks like," I said.

She nodded and winked. "Sexy. Is that what you mean?"

I hadn't thought of him like that. He was just a cute and successful guy that I liked and admired. And flats might be a comfortable change.

"Is he staying with you this time, cookie?" Lynda asked with a sly grin. She caught me for the gazillionth time. I liked and hated that Lynda knew me so well. I had to admit, it saved a lot of explaining and hiding.

When Gary mentioned that he would stay in a hotel, as he had in the past, I'd nixed the idea and assured him that he should use the guest bedroom.

"We're big kids," I'd said. He'd laughed some, which made me wonder if he thought we weren't or if he had another plan. I was always in a rush to get to the next step. Patience had never been a friend of mine.

Gary smiled and waved when he saw me at the gate. He put his bag down, pulled me into his arms, and hugged me. No kiss. But before my mind could run away with wild thoughts, he started to tell me about the guy who'd been sitting next to him on the plane.

"Rob was his name. Big and muscle-bound. The kind you might cross the street to avoid. Anyway, turns out he was flying down to Phoenix to pick up a chihuahua for his girlfriend's birthday. He was wringing his hands the whole trip."

I frowned. "Did I miss something? Why was he upset?"

Gary continued, "He's afraid of little dogs. When he was a toddler some small dog bit him and he had to have stitches. I'm nervous for the dog on the trip back to Seattle."

We had a good belly laugh.

"Hey speaking of pets," Gary said, "how's Prince?"

The cat had been doing strange things that brought joy into my otherwise routine life. Lately he had taken up with the kids next door, and one day he'd walked to school with them. When he loitered outside the building, the janitor looked at the information on his collar and called me saying that he thought the cat was lost. I assured him that Prince would come home when he got bored, which he did.

"Prince wanders all over town," I said. "He is truly a curious cat. Treats are at my door every night when I get home from work."

Gary said he wanted to do some tourist stuff on his visit. "Maybe see one of those western theme towns where they have gunfights. Or take a ride out in the desert and look for snakes."

I rolled my eyes. "It is your vacation. Trust me, though: once you see a snake you'll be sorry you did. And a gunfight? It's like watching a movie."

All of my work friends who had children frequented Rawhide, the mock western town in Scottsdale that looked like a movie set. Tourists raved about it. Obviously the heat affected their judgment. When I described it in detail to Gary, I didn't disclose that I had never set foot in the parking lot.

We drove to Rawhide the next day. Buses parked haphazardly: cars clogged the rutted and stony field. Dust coated our shoes as we walked to the entrance where dozens waited to buy tickets from a man dressed up like an old-time sheriff. A dummy with a rifle slumped in a chair next to the hitching post but moved just as we got to the ticket booth. I jumped a mile and everyone around us roared. The dummy tipped his hat before resuming his dead man pose.

"Was this guy here the last time you came?" Gary said. I started to answer until I noticed his arched eyebrow. "Busted," he said. "You're busted."

There's a reason tourist traps survive. Proprietors give the tourists exactly what they expect, with plenty of humor thrown in for insurance. No one seems to care if the jokes are stale or the situations well-rehearsed and contrived. Still, the gunfight Gary and I attended at the Okay Corral was more fun than I dreamed it could be, especially when they pulled a dad from Iowa out of the crowd. He stole the show so completely that Gary and I finally decided he was a plant. Later, we rode burros that had their own idea of which way to go. We nibbled on "Jesse James" burgers and washed them down with icy beers. We stopped on our way out of Rawhide to have our picture taken in western garb. Gary looking mean, like a gunslinger, and me dressed up as a saloon girl waving a 45 with my leg propped up on a chair. Years later, friends who saw the picture would comment that I looked like the one who'd shoot you off your horse.

That night we dined with Lynda, and she was on full throttle. She told Gary she had taken a nap so she could stay out late.

"I'm Nancy's almost-mother, but don't worry Gary," she said. "She may be a tough cookie in business, but she's a marshmallow. And I think she may have a crush."

My face and neck lit up crimson. I wanted to kill her. Gary laughed and smiled at me. It didn't affect him negatively. He nodded; he seemed to like it.

Gary encouraged Lynda to talk, an approach that was always a sure winner. She loved to tell stories from her past, and the degree to which she enhanced them depended on the listener's attention and the time she had available. Gary gave her both. The more we laughed, the funnier she became.

"There's definitely a future for you in stand-up comedy," Gary told her.

"He's much cuter than you said, Nancy." Lynda turned to me. "And so sharp."

The first bottle of wine didn't last fifteen minutes. Gary motioned to the waiter to bring another, and we rolled our way through appetizers, salad, and entrees. Finally Lynda started to slow down.

"You should get out more," I said to her. "Think what it would do for the economy."

That opened the door for Lynda to discuss politics—never a favorite subject of mine. She had a penchant for critical commentary of both parties. "They all stink" she liked to say.

"What's the political scene like in Seattle?" she asked.

Gary explained the city's liberal history, its long alignment with the Democratic Party. She leaned in and rested her chin in her hands. Before he finished she quizzed him on his stand.

"Fiscally conservative, socially liberal," Gary answered.

Her shoulders relaxed and she sat back in her seat. "I like that. It sums up exactly how I would describe myself."

That night, Gary headed for the guest bedroom but stopped and turned. He motioned toward my room. "That's where I'd really like to be," he said.

The feeling was mutual. Lying next to him felt good and safe. Passion was part of the puzzle as well, but different from how it had been with others. Lovemaking took time and happened gently. Almost as if he thought I'd break.

Each night we went to bed earlier and slept later. While I ran in the morning, he collected oranges from the backyard and squeezed them for juice. He played with Prince while he read the newspaper, even though he maintained he disliked cats. I knew right away the four-day escape would end too quickly.

He held me in his arms at the airport. I didn't want him to leave. I wanted to belong to someone, a real guy. As independent as I claimed to be, the single life wore me down. I hated starting over every few months. And dating several men at once never worked for me. Anyone can get a date, but I yearned for roots.

"It'll work out," he said. "We just need some time." I let go of my breath and swallowed. He stood back from me still holding one of my hands. His eyes locked on me for several seconds.

The words surprised me. Could I trust him? He had nothing to gain by making false predictions. Nothing about him seemed phony.

"He's a teddy bear," Lynda said. "I wanted to hug him. And that mischievous grin."

She walked around my condo in Phoenix with a two-by-four-foot picture in her hands, holding it up on the wall in various locations. She had promised to give me the collectable pen-and-ink drawing of the Grand Canyon that she claimed she no longer needed once I got settled. I jumped at the chance to have her hang it, as she had a good eye for that. Finally it claimed a spot near the fireplace. She propped it up, then stood back to inspect from several viewpoints.

"So you liked Gary? You approve?" I said.

"The fact that Robin likes him so much is the acid test," she said as she started to hammer in the hook. I watched without really paying attention. "And he likes her as well. Plus, Prince likes him. What do you need? Approval stamped in blood?"

I didn't tell her what Gary had said to me at the airport. It might jinx the whole thing. Dreams of a life with him filled my head. But a life where?

"Have you ever been to Seattle, Lynda?" I said.

She continued to inspect her picture-hanging project. Sometimes she would think of an even better solution long after I thought she was finished. "Decorating is ongoing" was her motto.

"Moss grows on your ying-yang. But yes, of course, I've been there. Boeing airplanes and that department store everyone talks about—Nordstrom."

I laughed at her ability to condense any subject down to one sentence. She had traveled extensively and always managed to absorb interesting facts. I enjoyed the challenge of trying to add something she hadn't thought of.

"What about Mt. Rainier?" I said.

"What about it? It's a big mountain. Something I'd admire only from the bottom," she said.

"Did you like it there, in Seattle?" I asked. She nodded, albeit slowly. "It's green. A million shades of green and hilly."

We put away the decorating supplies: tape measure, nails, hammer, and step ladder. She watched me return each item to its proper place in a well-organized drawer. She grinned. I realized I'd picked up this organizing skill from her.

"This is serious with Gary, yes?" Lynda said. I didn't respond but she knew the answer. "How do you know he wouldn't move down here?"

A good question but logic told me he had power in Seattle. It had taken him three years to gain the trust and respect of the navy and the university. No doubt the payoff had just started and promised to continue. Not an investment a salesman would want to give up.

My new romance dominated my conversations with Lynda. If we weren't debating the wisdom of me embarking on yet another relationship, we were discussing the pros and cons of me leaving Arizona. Lynda wanted me to stay and Gary to move, no matter how often I explained the problem with that.

"I'm thinking of moving, myself," she said one day. At first I thought she meant out of state, and it shocked me. She had loved Arizona for so long I couldn't imagine her being happy any place else.

"Ahwatukee is a new adult community southeast of Tempe," she said. "There's golf, tennis, and it's affordable." Nothing about her lifestyle suggested an adult community where I envisioned the residents coming together for bingo and shuffleboard. She assured me the place was nothing like that. I demanded a tour.

"It is so far away I feel like we're in Casa Grande," I said on the day she took me. The area had only a few stores, one office building, and acres upon acres of raw land. The golf course had rolling green fairways, sand traps, and baby trees. The temporary clubhouse consisted of manufactured buildings connected via a breezeway. The whole thing signaled second-rate to me. I shook my head in silent disbelief that she was considering moving there.

From the clubhouse she moved me to the sales office. She raved about the model development as we inspected what would be. Fully developed, the community would be dense and forgettable. Lynda pointed out three available seven thousand-square-foot lots for her prospective home. She had lived in spacious custom homes for over twenty years. All the patio homes she showed me were two bedroom, two bath, and under two thousand square feet. The exteriors were all the same color with one of three different facades. Each house had one tree and limited desert landscaping ... no grass.

"So which lot do you like the best?" she said with a big grin. "And don't you agree it will be most pleasant on the golf course?"

I couldn't feign excitement. The place was cheap, cheap, cheap. What in the world would she have in common with others who lived here? And exactly who would want to live here? I predicted a regrettable decision.

"Lynda, let's head back to town for lunch. My treat," I said. She looked confused and disappointed.

"You don't like the place, do you, cookie?" she said as we walked to the car. "Maybe you don't understand what I'm trying to accomplish."

Her words stonewalled me. She continued toward my Monte Carlo without talking or glancing my way. A heavy scowl revealed her anger.

She's right. What do I know?

We had supported each other's decisions in the past. If one of us didn't understand the other's circumstances, we took time to explain. Mutual respect forged our bond. I had violated our unspoken agreement.

I started the car and then turned it off. Lynda glanced over at me with tears in her eyes.

"My money is dwindling faster than you can drain a bath tub. I don't know what else to do. Maybe I should consider a trailer park," she said.

"What? How did this happen? What about the money in Mexico?" I said. The information shook me. She exaggerated so frequently, maybe this was one of those times.

"I'm not sure I'll ever see the money in Mexico. I've actually been trying to get some of it out," she said softly. "Right now I'd settle for having half of it back."

What could I say? Her investment advisor and accountant had cautioned her against putting money there. She thought she knew better and that she'd show them a thing or two about a good return on her money. I remembered when she bragged that she'd have the last laugh.

"I feel so stupid. They'll say I deserve this," she said.

We sat in silence. I had no advice, no words of encouragement or hope. It had been my impression that she had millions.

"Of your net worth—how much is in Mexico?" I said.

"One third," she said. "It was the return I needed to live on. Now I don't have the return or the principal."

Discussion about money was new territory for us. It left me uncomfortable. She came across as wanting to share details that I didn't want to know. Was I the only one she confided in? Her circumstances were completely outside of my experience. As private as she was about her personal affairs to others, she had become an open book to me.

"I could cash out and live out here okay," she said as she gazed out the window. "You could come visit. George and I would have miles of sidewalk to explore. It could be worse."

After a while we pulled ourselves together. Her left eye twitched. I laid a hand on her arm. "You can make anything work, that I do know," I said.

She glimpsed at me and then back out the window to an empty parking lot and construction vehicles in the distance. I wasn't sure she digested my words. Maybe it didn't matter.

"Where shall I take you to lunch?"

She shrugged. "Not that hungry. Maybe another time."

We didn't discuss Ahwatukee for a week. I decided that I'd wait for her to bring it up. Perhaps she would map out another financial plan to save herself from a move to the hinterland. She was smart and resourceful. Her ability to survive was her most defining trait.

How's the hip?" I asked one day. She wasn't limping and her sunny smile had returned on occasion.

"I'm doing some exercises and taking it easy," she said. "I miss those bitches at the tennis court. Who'd have thought I'd ever say that?" She giggled.

"You miss the women or the competition?"

"Door number two of course," she said. "They're all younger and better athletes, but I was more patient and practiced. What great fun to surprise them. And the strenuous exercise kept the pounds off. Now I practically have to weigh everything I put in my mouth."

"Gary is coming to Phoenix again," I said. "He wants to take us both out to dinner. Let's do something in Scottsdale."

She poured us some of her gourmet coffee. "Maybe he wants to ask me for your hand in marriage. He knows I'm your almost-mother." Sweat broke out on my forehead. Lynda had a way of figuring out my biggest fears and making me face them.

"He likes you, that's all," I said. "No other reason."

I started getting excited the week before he arrived. Nights were restless, and I began to cross off days the way a kid does before Christmas. The time dragged until he finally walked off the plane and into my arms. We hugged and kissed, then kissed some more.

We played miniature golf, raced go-karts, saw a movie, made dinner, and enjoyed Lynda's company. Each time he visited, it was as if he were treating me to a vacation in my own home town. I wondered how he found out so much about Phoenix, but I never got around to asking him. I was lost in my emotions, feeling loved for the first time in years. Before he left, Gary invited me to Seattle for Thanksgiving and to meet his family.

"Uh-oh," Lynda said. "You know what that means. And November in Seattle—it'll be raining sideways."

As much as Robin liked Gary, she didn't warm up to the idea of me going to Seattle. "He should come to Phoenix," she said as if to claim it as her home. "You aren't moving there, are you?"

Everyone speculated on my trip plans. Joe told everyone at work that I had a new boyfriend—one who had already graduated from college.

Mom reminded me that I had been to Seattle as a teenager. "That train trip you took to California with Lilly when you were a teenager, I think you changed trains there," she said.

How did she remember that? I had taken that vacation with grandma almost twenty years earlier.

"I don't think that's enough to count," I said. "Anyway, the train station is downtown and Gary lives on the east side, the suburbs."

Mom wanted more information, but most of her questions were about things I wanted to know: what his mother was like, whether his siblings were nice, if he was a neat person, how he lived day-to-day. I was about to hang up when she said, "Why did he and his wife get divorced?"

It was a question I'd heard frequently after Sam and I ended our marriage. It irked me. I couldn't believe how brazen people were, or fathom why they thought they even had a right to ask. One of my friends pointed out that perhaps women thought if it happened to me it could happen to them. She added that they might be trying to keep from making a mistake that could cost them.

"Gary said that they were too young, only nineteen, and it became clear that they weren't on the same path," I said. Even though Gary had told me they had split over a disagreement over whether to have children, I didn't share that information.

So many subjects had become difficult in my conversations with Lynda: the possible move to po-dunk village, her deteriorating back and hip, my long-distance romance and then she added a bomb: "Tim dropped out of ASU," she said one afternoon.

We had just come in from an afternoon stroll with George. She was moving slower and slower, the way someone who was afraid of falling might walk. I suspected intense pain that she masked. She claimed that being intensely careful of everything in her path was critical.

I stomped my foot. "No, no. Tim didn't."

"What in the world have I done right?" she said. "I feel so failed."

"Did he say why?" I said.

"College isn't for me. I don't need it," she said, using Tim's voice. We shared a cynical smirk and motioned George toward the house.

I knew that studying and discipline weren't high of Tim's to-do list, whereas procrastination was right at the top. Twice I had tried to reason with him about keeping up with his classes and studying some every day. He'd eyed me as if I were a lecturing parent.

"Were his grades bad?" I said.

She sneered. "You could guess, right? He was failing and not by just a little. I'm sure he dropped out now to avoid total humiliation."

"What about the gold mine investment? And what in the heck will he do if he's not in school?"

"Gold mine my ass," she said. "That money is totally gone, maybe the only idea worse than my Mexican money market account. He claims he can make a fortune as a bartender at Avanti's."

I sensed Tim's potential slipping away. I had never known anyone who so wanted fame and fortune without expecting to have to work for it. I couldn't decide if he suffered from an inferiority or a superiority complex. Maybe both. I wished I could think of something to alleviate Lynda's guilt. Her life looked bleak, while mine had turned a corner and begun rising. Nothing horrible threatened my dawn.

"I guess we balance each other out—the good and the bad news," she muttered. I started to disagree, but she put a finger to her lips.

Thanksgiving in Seattle was magical. The rain held off for half the visit, and somehow it didn't seem that cold, even if Gary kept the gas fireplace on for my entire visit and I wore every sweater I owned.

We spent Thanksgiving day with Gary's siblings and mother in her brick ranch house in Tacoma. His two older siblings were married with children. Small children were always a challenge for me, but the four of them, whose ages ranged from five to ten, were a delight to be around. Even better, everyone treated me as a relative, instead of a guest. Funny family stories were told all around. Even Momma Elaine entered in with a Thanksgiving toast: "And we give thanks that Gary has finally found a girlfriend who isn't a cocktail waitress." That got such a big laugh Gary's face turned bright red.

When I asked Elaine how long she had lived in the house, everyone chimed in to tell the story of how the family had moved in after it was built in 1960. They had all been excited to live in a brand new, three-bedroom home. Elaine had been there ever since.

"Three bedrooms. How did that work with five kides?"

Elaine laughed. "Two sets of bunk beds in one room for all the boys, then Marianne had her room, as did Bud and I.

"Wow, sound crowded," I said. Then I added, "But it looks like everyone turned out okay."

"Except for Dean," Gary said. "He's still a little weird." We all laughed, especially Dean.

Lynda waved at me in baggage claim. Her winter white wool pants and pale yellow cashmere sweater showcased her red hair. Her hands were raised well over her head and she practically jumped up and down. Nothing about her was subtle. A few people smiled at her exuberance.

"I missed you, cookie," she said and hugged me. "So much has happened while you were gone. But first tell me—are you engaged? Do you have to move? Are you still in love?"

"Whoa, slow down. No, no, and yes," I said.

We waited at the carousel for my luggage. She hugged me again. "I think you'll approve this time," she said.

I stood back. "You bought a house in Ahwatukee?"

"It really will be fine," she said. "Honest. I feel much better about the whole thing and it came in less than I budgeted, even with all the upgrades. John went with me to finalize the deal."

My suitcase slid down the chute and I grabbed it. No matter how good the vacation had been, it felt good to be home. I had a sudden urge to see Prince and pet him for a while.

"What was the most fun thing you did in Seattle?" Lynda asked, shaking me out of thoughts of the cat.

I had to think about it. Gary had wined and dined me every day. The delicious Thanksgiving ranked right up there as well. It might have been easier if she asked me what had been so-so on the trip.

"Dinner on top of the space needle," I said. "It moves around while you eat."

"Oh my god," she said. "That sounds awful."

I laughed. "It's so slow you aren't even aware. I think it took an hour to make one rotation. The view is spectacular from several hundred feet. You see Puget Sound and the city in all directions."

When we got to her car, she tuned the radio to KUPD just as Crazy Dave launched into his favorite subject, the ASU football coach who'd been fired for punching a student. "I think after all the fiasco with hitting the kid," Dave was saying, "Frank Kush should change his name to Frank Crush."

Lynda shook her head. "The worst of it is that the kid probably deserved it. Too bad they caught it on camera. It'll be his downfall, even if he has been there twenty years."

"So what all happened while I was gone? You said lots of stuff," I said as I nudged her.

She turned the radio off but didn't say a word. It spooked me a little. I craned my neck to get a better look at her face.

"They can't do anything for my hip, not really. Just as I believed. Or, just as I feared," she muttered. "The back and neck are the real problems. Dr. Russo referred me to a pain management specialist. What a crock."

The stillness in the car made me aware of every engine noise. I wanted to give her hope. Nothing came to mind.

"With a different narcotic and a cane, I might be able to walk George. That's about as much as I can hope for." She smirked.

As soon as Lynda pulled into my driveway, Prince sprung from two units away. It made her smile.

"He's such a love," she said.

Prince lagged behind us into the condo and then immediately raced up the stairs. Lynda's eyes followed.

"He seems to get a kick out of going up and down," I said.

"My worst nightmare," Lynda said. "On a brighter note, I met with the Ahwatukee sales agent, Coleen, and picked out colors, carpets, and tile. The project gives me something to look forward to. I could have waited until you got back, but I needed diversion. Plus Coleen is a sharp woman with good taste. I enjoy the time I spend with her."

It was past time for debate. Maybe she was right—the move could be positive. Having greater financial security might relieve some of her stress, and anyway, maybe I had underestimated the appeal of the place.

"When do you think you'll be moving?" I asked her.

"Next fall."

She bent down to scratch Prince's head and then groaned. He sidled up against her leg.

Within a short time, Gary announced that he'd like to spend Christmas in Arizona with me. Lynda loved the news and so did Robin.

"One big almost-family," Lynda said. "I'll make the holiday dinner. Prime rib and Yorkshire pudding are my specialty."

How strange will that be?

She convinced me that I'd be too busy with Gary, Robin, and presents to worry about preparing a meal. Later, I realized she had offered to cook as a distraction for herself and also to give herself a fun place to be on Christmas. She had already shared that Tim was going to Colorado to be with his uncle.

"No one I'd rather be with than the three of you," she told me. "What shall I get Robin? I want it to be a total surprise. And speaking of surprises, dahling Nancy: what do you think Gary is getting you?"

I had pondered that one, myself.

Gary said he'd come to Phoenix two days before Christmas. "We'll have time alone and to get ready for Robin. Don't decorate the tree until I get there," he added. "I love that part."

Before he arrived, I bought the tree and set it up in its stand. He had been right; I should have waited for his help. Trying to get it upright and straight was as difficult as it was comical. Prince lounged on the couch and watched the struggle. I swore and laughed but the anticipation of being surrounded by all my favorite people for the holiday overshadowed any dilemma. It was hard to finger all of my childhood ornaments without hanging them up. The memory of my Grandmother Lilly and all the wonderful Christmas dinners at her brick Tudor in Cleveland Heights came back to me. Lilly had snow-white hair and rosy cheeks, and her enormous blue eyes sparkled behind glasses. Her girth suited the jovial woman. All six of her young grandchildren told her at one point or another how much she looked like Mrs. Claus. "Maybe I am," she would say. "My secret life, for part of the year."

It was time to make my own traditions, not just for me, but for Robin. Whenever I talked with Robin about my favorite relatives, Lilly among them, she'd scrunch up her face. "They died before I was born," she'd say, as if I'd forgotten. I assured her that someday she'd want to know more about her ancestors and their family customs. That conversation usually ended with a shrug and heavy sigh on her part.

When Gary arrived, he and I sipped wine, listened to Christmas carols, and decorated the tree. He wanted to hear about the people and traditions I associated with the ornaments. My stories seemed to jog his own memories of his favorite relatives and traditions.

"I think your grandma Lilly was better than my Nana," he said. "Mine was the kind who'd give you a fire truck as a present but tell you to play with it when you got home."

"C'mon," I said, "she didn't really say that. You're exaggerating just to make a good story."

He jabbed me. "You should know."

We separated strands of tinsel and finished off the stately pine. Gary turned on the tree lights and flipped off the living room lamps. We lay on the carpet and stared up at the tree. It was the prettiest one I'd seen in years.

He tapped my arm. "What would you like for Christmas, if you could have anything at all?"

I can't tell him. I can't.

"There's No Place Like Home for the Holidays" played on the tape deck. I nodded at the sentiment. I was home, my home.

He tapped me again. "You can tell me. And none of that peace-on-earth goodwill toward men."

"I want the fairy tale," I said, barely aloud.

He nodded. "That's what I thought."

It surprised me. Did he really know what I meant? I had wanted to be truthful without really disclosing my wish.

Robin was the first person off the plane, along with the stewardess who accompanied her. She jumped up and down.

"Mommy. Gary," she said. "Mary gave me my wings."

She pointed to the pin on her jacket. The stewardess smiled and gave her a quick hug good-bye.

"What a great kid you have," she said. Robin beamed up at her.

We strolled toward baggage claim while Robin rehashed the five-hour flight in vivid detail. I pretended to listen but watched Gary devour all the particulars. She knew she had his ear and prolonged the story.

I now know where she gets it.

He chuckled at something she said and took her hand. She swung her arm back and forth, comfortable with him. I felt like an interested bystander.

"What should we have for Christmas Eve dinner?" Gary said to Robin. She scratched her head like she needed to think it over.

"Cheeseburgers, cheeseburgers," she said, "but not like those burnt ones you made me last time."

"Good memory, bad scene," Gary said.

Christmas morning didn't start until ten. Robin had never been one of those kids who wakes up at the crack of dawn, even for the biggest morning of the year. Gary and I enjoyed coffee and played with Prince while she slept. He caught me eying the presents under the tree.

"Want to guess what I got you?" he said.

One box looked like a blouse or sweater, another one was six inches square, and a third was the size of a notebook. The only one that held my attention was the square.

"When I was a kid, I used to burrow into Mom's hiding places, unwrap and then rewrap my presents. It sure made Christmas morning a disappointment," I said.

"Good to know," Gary said, "although that doesn't surprise me one bit. She never figured it out?"

"Oh yeah, she found better hiding places. Then, as much as I liked the hunt of trying to find the gifts, I had a much better time on Christmas morning. I've probably outgrown such juvenile behavior, no?"

He shook his head and laughed. "I wouldn't trust you."

Robin shuffled into the kitchen. She rubbed her eyes. "Merry Christmas, Mom, Gary."

We all moved toward the tree and the overly generous pile of gifts for three people. Robin's grandmothers and other relatives had forwarded their gifts for her to me.

"Most of these are for you," I said.

She grinned. "I know. Last night I snuck in here and looked at the name tags. Wow. I don't think I've ever had fourteen. I hope they aren't all clothes. Remember those socks with the toes that Aunt Junie got me last year? Sometimes I get weird stuff like that, and I'm not a kid anymore. I'm nine!"

"Uh oh," Gary said. Robin nudged him. "You didn't get me that did you? You're teasing me again, right?"

Gary reached under the tree and pulled out a box with an oversized red bow. It had no name tag.

"I wondered who that one was for," Robin said. She sat on the floor with her legs curled up underneath her Indian style and rocked back and forth.

She pulled the ribbon off in one yank and tore through the paper. "Wow. Etch a Sketch. I love it. Thanks, Gar."

The directions fell out of the box. She turned knobs every which way. "Cool, look what I did," she giggled. "Oops, that's not right."

I suggested she take a look at the instructions but she ignored me and continued the exploration unguided. My mother used to tell me that one day I would be repaid for all my stubbornness. Gary and I exchanged a knowing look.

Robin also received an Arizona State sweatshirt, dozens of stickers to add to her collection, books, a jewelry box that played music, pajamas, a chess set, raincoat, and more. She buried herself amidst boxes without losing a big smile.

Gary opened a cashmere sweater, a framed picture of the two of us, *Jonathan Livingston Seagull*, and a keychain with his initials. I got a silk blouse, a suede leather wallet/checkbook, and fuzzy slippers. Finally only one gift remained, the square one from Gary to me.

"Now do you want to guess?" he asked. I shook my head but Robin raised her hand. "I will," she said as she took the box from Gary and shook it. "It's light, like there's nothing in it," she said. "I give up. Open it, Mom."

Glossy red paper and a green bow piqued my curiosity. Robin was right—it was as light as an empty box. Inside, there were layers of tissue paper and finally a Christmas ornament. A house with "The Rossmans" printed on its roof. I pulled it out and squinted.

Uh?

"What do you think?" Gary said as he moved closer to me.

It made no sense. I couldn't think of a thing to say. Robin took the ornament out of my hand and inspected it.

"I don't understand," I said.

Gary coughed. "Okay, too subtle. I want you to be a part of my house, as my wife. Will you marry me?"

Robin screamed. "Yes, yes she will. But you have to move here, Gary. I hear it rains every day in Seattle."

Tears followed each other silently down my cheeks. We hugged. Robin joined in.

The rest of the visit was spent selling Robin on the benefits of Seattle. Gary put all his skills to use, answering all of her objections with calmness and interest. "We'll buy a new house, one big enough for all of us and Prince," he said. "There are lots of parks where you can ride your bike, big lakes to swim in during the summer, good restaurants, and plenty of other kids to play with."

She argued for a while. "I like the sunshine in Arizona. We can swim all year, not just the summer."

Gary had nothing left. "Robin, I have a good career in Seattle. I'm sorry, but that's the way it is."

"Mom has a career too, and it's here," she said. Her lower lip quivered and then stayed stuck out. He took her hand and held it.

"Tell you what. I promise that we will always spend your spring vacation in Arizona. How's that?" he said.

A smile returned to her face. "Okay, but I still think you should get a career here in Arizona."

I told Gary I should be the one to break the news to Lynda, after he left. I had no idea how she'd react. We reminded Robin several times not to spill the beans.

Several hours later we headed over for the Christmas prime rib dinner. We had agreed earlier not to exchange gifts. When I had tentatively suggested this plan, Lynda quickly agreed. "But one for cookie II," she said. "I bought it last week. It's a winner."

"Merry Christmas, Lynda," Robin shouted as we arrived. She hugged Lynda around the waist and squeezed.

"Oh my, Robin. You're so strong today," she said. Gary and I kissed her and ambled toward the wonderful aromas lingering in the kitchen, while Robin wandered down the hall in search of George. Lynda raced into the living room and returned with a box big enough to hold a lamp. It was wrapped in gold foil and Christmas bows.

Robin gasped as she bounced into the room with George in close pursuit. "Wow. For me?" she grinned.

"Santa said you've been good. Well, actually he said you've been pretty good. So, yes, it is for you, dear girl," Lynda said.

Robin carefully removed all the bows, which amused Lynda. She even undid the wrapping with such caution, it could have been reused. She shook the box and it rattled slightly.

"A bowling ball?" she said. Lynda smiled. "An erector set?" We all laughed.

She pulled off the remaining tape and plowed through the tissue paper, and then peeked inside. "I love them," she shouted and pulled out white boots with white fur on the tops. The combination of white fur-trimmed boots with her ASU gym shorts and a sweatshirt made us giggle, but Robin could have cared less. She marched to Lynda's bedroom where she knew there was a full-length mirror.

"I'll be the coolest kid at Case Elementary," she yelled.

"Robin, there's more in the bottom of the box," Lynda said.

Robin could have set a sprint record back to the table. She turned the box upside down and a petite pink backpack with tons of zippers fell on the floor.

She picked it up and hugged it to her chest. "I love it, I love it."

Two days after Robin and Gary left, I decided I needed to share the news of the wedding and relocation. I worried about how Lynda would take it, or if she would be surprised.

We sat outside, sipping her delicious homemade sun tea. She was combing George, stopping every so often to pull excess hair out of the brush.

"The best Christmas I've had in a long time," Lynda said. "No family drama, no worry about appropriate gifts, and a wonderful prime rib dinner, even if I do pat myself on the back."

"We set a record for the most food consumed by four people," I said. "And you should congratulate yourself. I give you huge kudos."

She refocused her attention on George and inspected his fur for missed spots. I thought I heard her sigh.

"When are you getting married?" she said.

I cleared my throat. "Don't know about that yet, but he did ask me to marry him. I said yes. Robin knows and she seems to be thrilled about it. Of course, I want to apply for a transfer with Xerox, but that appears to be doable. And we'll need to figure out what furniture I'll move, and so on. Just details."

She nodded and stopped brushing. "He's a good guy Nancy. A very good guy."

I knew her compliment about Gary was sincere, but her ensuing silence made me uneasy.

"I'll be okay," she said, as if she had read my mind. "I'm sure I'll meet some nice folks in Ahwatukee once I move out there. That sales gal, Coleen, predicts I'll have all sorts of things in common with the people who are buying. The change will be good for me. I can start playing golf again."

"New outfits," I exclaimed. "But listen, how good are you, anyhow?"

She gave George a pat to let him know he could run off.

"I strive for bogey golf in a great-looking outfit," she said. "Maybe we could get in some rounds before you head out of town. How much time do we have?"

"October, I think. Weather-wise I should be going this summer. Won't happen, though—too much planning to do."

October seemed forever away. We would have ten months to do everything Lynda wanted. My friendship with her had become such a big part of my life, we were nearly co-dependent. The role she played in my life would in some sense transfer to Gary if we were to have the kind of marriage I wanted. Who would step in to fill my place in Lynda's life? I thought of Nora, her friend from years before. Maybe I could help resurrect that friendship. Geography alone seemed to be the reason they had drifted apart: Nora and her husband lived on a big ranch outside Nogales, Arizona, and both women had dropped out of the horse business after Peter died. A 150-mile commute would alter any friendship, but I believed that both of them stood to benefit from a reconnection. Then there was also Tim, who might step back in once Lynda got over his decision to drop out of college. She had become accustomed to companionship, which she probably needed more than she wanted to acknowledge.

Meanwhile, Ahwatukee became the focus for Lynda's future. I decided to adjust my thinking by joining her there for the construction update and design meetings. Excitement and optimism are contagious: certainly I could be the catalyst that gave her hope for a future filled with pleasant people and activities. To put myself in the right mindset, I imagined myself in her shoes. Life hadn't gone the way I planned either, and who knew what boulders loomed in the future. It was time to show my enthusiasm for her choice.

The more trips we made to Ahwatukee, the more positive things I found. Signs for upcoming development began to pop up. Travel to and from Tempe didn't seem to take as long. We checked out the master plan each time we met with Coleen, to see how many more lots had sold. The number of sales shocked both of us. Where were all the people coming from?

Lynda pored over building plans for weeks. She measured furniture and came up with several ways to lay out the various rooms. Some of her concoctions were too bizarre for my taste. I tried to be supportive and not offer advice unless she asked for my opinion.

"All the exteriors look so much the same, I'll have to count the houses to make sure I get to my garage," she joked. "That's why I want my inside to be completely different from what anyone else would do."

"I think you're safe," I said.

The project began to consume so much of our time, it bothered me. In a way, it seemed that she might be putting too much thought—even too much hope—into her new life. Coleen must have tired of the daily phone calls because it didn't take long before she was always in a meeting whenever Lynda called. Sometimes the phone call went unreturned for two days. It drove Lynda nuts.

"No customer service," she griped. "As soon as my deposit was non-refundable, she disappeared."

I felt Coleen's pain. A sales career wasn't made up of big commissions and often the selling process continued long after the order was placed. Difficult customers, like Lynda, had a never-ending list of concerns, almost as if they were permanently stuck in buyer's remorse.

"Coleen has gone the extra mile in this deal," I finally said. "Not much happens in a day. It's not her job to inspect what did or didn't happen each and every day—she's not in construction, she's a sales agent."

The line went quiet for so long that I thought Lynda had hung up on me. I out-waited her.

"You think I'm annoying her?" Lynda said.

"Yes," I said.

More silence. Again, I waited. If I had learned nothing else in my years of selling, I had learned patience. It hadn't happened overnight or without conscious effort. I practiced. My sales manager had drummed his mantra it into all of us: "Any time you make a powerful statement, end it with silence. Shut up and wait. The first one to talk loses."

Lynda groaned. "Okay, cookie, if you say so. I know you're only trying to help me. And how brave you are to stick your neck out when I mess up."

I considered whether she really meant it. Probably she wanted to, but Lynda usually didn't respond well to criticism. Who does? I was unusual in that regard: whatever defensiveness I had left me after a year or so in sales. Constant critique became essential to my growth and success, and this spilled over into my personal life in a good way. Mostly I wanted truth, which saved time and tap dancing in the long run. Still, I learned the hard way that no matter how much others said they wanted the truth, they seldom were prepared to accept it.

Lynda began reaching out to John and Janet. She told me of phone calls and dinner plans. I knew that she was preparing for others to fill the void I would leave. Perhaps she thought that hosting dinners at trendy restaurants would create a neutral territory where they could begin to reconnect. When she reported conversations from various outings, they sounded encouraging. I considered whether John and Janet were being nice to her because they liked the free food. Still, I congratulated her for making the effort.

An even better solution would be for Tim to get his act together. That connection had been good from the start, and I knew she missed him terribly. Their disconnect had been recent, a result of his poor investment choices and irresponsible behavior. She couldn't keep from giving advice that he didn't want to hear. He quit calling while she fumed.

Meanwhile, Gary and I saw each other every two or three weeks. The weather in Phoenix was a welcome reprieve for him and I blossomed in his attention. We talked about how we would merge our houses and when. He thought we should sell all of my things and just move me, Prince, and my personal items. At first it irritated me, but he did have better furniture and the cost of moving all of mine was impractical. He let me chew on the idea for a couple of weeks without pushing. The main thing we agreed on was to sell my condo. Phoenix had been cheap for a long time, but real estate was starting to ratchet up. Lynda had hoped we'd keep the condo so that we'd visit more often, but it really didn't make financial sense. I quit discussing my plans with her when I noticed her agitation.

"We should take a trip to Nogales so that you can meet my friend Nora," she said one day. I jumped at the idea, somewhat startled that she had brought it up when I had been thinking the same thing. It didn't take a day to firm up some plans for us to all meet at Rio Rico, a resort outside Nogales. The trip gave Lynda a shot of adrenaline and joy. She told me more about her history with Nora, during the good old days when they had both been involved with horse shows.

"Nora and I liked each other from the start. Kind of like you and me," she said. "Nora was the respected trainer and famous horse woman on the circuit while I wanted the thrill of the show as a rider. She taught me so much."

Lynda explained that horses were still Nora's greatest love but that she'd been out of the limelight for the past five years. Her increased back pain had worsened to the point that she finally had to make her health her top priority. Eventually, she'd retired, giving up the stable she'd run for years along with a waiting list of clients. Only Dolly remained, an old mare that had been her companion for years. Lynda said they were good company for each other.

The upcoming rendezvous sent Lynda scrambling through photo albums. We passed pictures of Nora, Lynda, and her late husband Peter back and forth. Riding clothes hadn't changed that much, and I thought Lynda looked smashing and modern in her garb. In two of the pictures, Nora held the reins of Bell with Lynda seated atop.

"That was a time," Lynda said. "How lucky to have had all that fun and attention, not to take away anything from Bell. He was a magnificent animal."

He stood proud and confident, his toned muscles glistening in the sun. There must have been a breeze as his tail flared out behind him. Lynda's posture mirrored his poise. I wondered if she truly had been so sure of herself back then.

"You were never afraid?" I said.

She tilted her head as if considering my question. "I only worried about him. More horses get hurt jumping than riders. It did take some time to let that go. A horse knows if you're afraid."

"Tell me about it," I said. "Dad used to say the same thing when he tried to get me to ride our wild ponies. I always responded with, 'Of course they know I'm afraid ... they're right!' Fear never left me."

I picked up a picture of Nora and studied it. She was slender, but there didn't appear to be anything else particularly attractive about her. No smile, very cowgirl, without style in her hair or clothing. She didn't seem a match for Lynda, which made me more curious.

"Two weeks, right? I'm really looking forward to this," I said. Lynda nodded and began putting all the mementos away.

Lynda must have phoned Nora every day the week before the trip. She repeated all of the plans they discussed. Nora decided at the last minute not to stay at the resort with us but to join us each day at lunch and spend the entire day. They agreed to take one day to cross into Nogales and visit some of their favorite haunts. Lynda spoke a weird kind of pidgin Spanish, but Nora was fluent.

"Can Nora sing the Spanish songs as well as you?" I said. Lynda shook her head. "She can salsa dance very well, though."

"And then there's me," I said. "I can't do either thing."

"It's okay," she assured me. "We need someone to be in the audience."

5

NORA

W E ARRIVED AT Rio Rico well ahead of schedule. The resort had been conceived by naïve Arizona real estate developers. The idea was that wealthy Mexicans would venture north across the border to stay at a fancy resort. People from Phoenix, meanwhile, would travel into Mexico to shop for cheap goods but not want to stay there. They would travel back into Arizona and stop at the resort instead of continuing more than 150 miles north to Phoenix. It sounded good in theory—two pools of tourists to draw from. The problem was that there was nothing in the area except the resort. In reality, wealthy Mexicans bypassed it for a city, and people in Phoenix yearned for charm in the surrounding area, more like the artist community of Tubac. The occupancy rate never hit a respectable number and continued to dwindle as the resort aged and quickly lost the appeal of being new. Still, even if the place was under-used, it was beautiful.

The driveway wound up the side of a large hill, otherwise known in Arizona as a mountain. The elevation gave the entrance pizzazz and drama. The bright white stucco buildings had tiled roofs and lapis blue awnings. The same lapis blue appeared in tiled arches and around windows. Fuchsia bougainvillea vines that had been pruned like trees scaled the walls. Courtyard fountains and potted ferns were everywhere. The whole thing had a Mediterranean feel.

"I love it," I said. "I could live here."

We had almost two hours to unpack, cruise the grounds, take a swim and lounge by the spectacular mosaic tiled pool before Nora was scheduled to arrive for our 1 p.m. lunch. In no time we were poolside in our bikinis, ordering lemonades.

"Too early for the margaritas," Lynda said. I had to agree, but the thought had crossed my mind. A slight breeze kept me from getting too hot as I stretched my legs in a padded lounge chair. The drive had made me sleepy. Lynda must have noticed my head bobbing because she quit talking all of the sudden and that reprieve let me drift off.

"Nora, you're early!" I woke up confused and dazed. Lynda was racing toward a woman at the far end of the pool.

From a distance, they could have been young girls hugging after a long absence. Nora jumped up and down, her ponytail swaying from side to side. *Ponytail.* Lynda kissed Nora on the cheek and then again.

I started to get up from the lounge chair and then hesitated. As much as I was dying to meet Nora, I didn't want to interrupt the reunion. They needed some private time to reconnect. After several minutes they glanced my way. Lynda took Nora's hand and they headed toward me.

"Nora, it's an honor to meet you," I said. "I can't wait to hear all the stories from your point of view."

She laughed. "I think you'll discover that both of us can tell a good tale," she said.

Lynda pulled up another lounge chair and Nora unzipped her jeans and stepped out. She wore a one-piece black bathing suit, very conservative except for the plunging neckline. Lynda had told me that they were the same age, fifty-two. Somehow Nora looked younger but I couldn't put my finger on why. She was taller than Lynda by five inches or so, meatier, but more toned and bronzed—probably because of all the time she spent outside with horses. She was much more attractive in person than in the photos I'd seen.

"The ranch will have to get along without me," Nora said. She motioned to a pool boy for a drink. "And not lemonade, a margarita, a big one with an extra shot and plenty of salt." He grinned.

Lynda slapped her thigh. "That's my Nora, always ready to start the party. I've told Nancy about our good old days."

"Oh darlin' and that's the truth. Such a couple of bad girls, it's a wonder we didn't have more injuries on those horses with all the partying we did." Nora leaned back into the chair and rubbed her temple. "By the way, Lynda, how is your neck? And spine?"

The pool boy returned with Nora's drink before Lynda had to answer. The margarita came in a mason jar crammed with ice, its rim thick with salt.

"Now you're talking," Nora said and flipped him a ten dollar bill. "Cheers, girls." She raised her glass toward us and took a big gulp.

It was the makings of a perfect day—good companions, agreeable weather, laughter, no commitments, all in a resort setting. For once I relaxed without an agenda or expectations. The new role appealed to me. I felt like I was on vacation with my older sisters, even though I didn't have any.

I could learn a ton.

"Ahhh," Nora closed her eyes and basked in the sun. Her red toe nails wriggled. "What shall we talk about first? Men? Mothers? Speaking of which, Lynda, is that old coot Marie still alive?"

"She'll go any day now, the doctor says, and frankly I'll be relieved. She's been a drain on my brain and my pocketbook," Lynda said.

Nora sat up. "Well, some people can be so cruel. No one would have been surprised if you refused to help her."

"I'm no saint," Lynda said. "There was no one else and I knew it, no matter what she deserved. I sent money instead of seeing her. It seemed like a fair deal."

Lynda pulled the *Arizona Republic* out of her beach bag and turned to the puzzle and comic section. "Cookie here has me doing the jumble and crossword every day," she said to Nora. "Want to help?"

Nora licked salt from the edge of the mason jar. "Not so much. If I ever have a minute I prefer a good book. Any recommendations?"

We chatted for a while before reverting back into our own worlds, comfortable in knowing we didn't have to entertain one another. Nora drifted off in no time, snoring slightly. An angelic face and a few freckles belied her years.

"She's so cute," I whispered to Lynda.

"Everyone says that."

Three women sharing one hotel room to shower and dress made for a great comedy scene. We ran back and forth in our underwear and jostled for space at the mirror as we put on finishing touches. Nora spent time on her eyes and almost nothing else. Lynda smoothed on foundation and light powder while I used two different brushes to even out the blush. Nora and I wore such pale pink lipstick that Lynda said it looked like we were bare. Nora leaned in closer to the mirror and turned her head left and then right. "Uh oh, there it is," she said. "My mother's face."

We giggled like teenagers, getting ready for a night out. My side ached from laughing.

Downstairs, to our surprise, the restaurant buzzed with activity.

"Food must be good if the locals are here," Nora said. Two Mexican men with guitars sidled past; one winked at her.

I nudged Lynda. "Maybe they're related to Carlos."

Nora knew there was a story. I recalled the scene at Westward Look, when Lynda earned her Oscar singing with Carlos. Lynda kept interrupting my exaggerated rendition until Nora silenced her.

"Oh let her tell it. This is hilarious. Who cares if it isn't entirely accurate? I love a good yarn."

Nora's laughter energized me. The story almost took longer to tell than the actual event had lasted. Lynda blushed and an unexpected shyness overtook her. She fidgeted with her silverware and avoided looking at either of us.

"I don't believe I've ever heard you sing. And I thought I knew everything about you," Nora said. "Let's get the men over here and do a replay."

Lynda shook her head violently. "That was a one-night wonder. I don't know what came over me. It's very possible I was just showing off."

Nora let it pass. We sampled each other's dinners and talked about our past lives and loves.

"So how's your marriage?" Lynda said.

"Ah, I wondered how long it'd be before you brought that up."

Nora cut into her steak and took a bite. She chewed and glanced down at her plate. "It's okay. Tolerable, very tolerable."

Wow. So honest.

Lynda sat back in her chair and studied her friend. Somehow the silence wasn't comfortable for me. I couldn't tell if Lynda didn't believe her or if she felt sorry for her. Nora, however, seemed satisfied.

"How long have you been married?" I asked.

Nora shrugged. "Thirty-one years." She leaned toward me. "There are stages in a marriage. I'm in the one where I've finally forgiven my husband for not being everything I wanted and accepted him for who he is."

"How wise of you," I said. "Do you miss the years of passion and obsession?"

"Passion is messy. Leon is easy to be with. He doesn't make unreasonable demands. At this point in my life, I want a good-natured personality and no drama. We still get together once in a while. Actually, separate bedrooms probably increased the desire in that department."

It all made sense but that was just the problem; emotion doesn't make sense. I wondered if she wished it were different. Maybe passion had never been there with Leon.

Lynda and Nora exchanged a look.

"Nancy's in the Cinderella era," Lynda said. Her words accurately described my desire, but they had a tinge of cynicism. I believed I could have romance forever. Passion left, I knew that, but wouldn't the depth of knowing and loving someone keep the fire burning?

I'd had a role model in my parents. Even if Mom had been in love before she met Dad, they were married twenty-four years before he died. They kissed a lot. Dad wrote poetry for her on each of their anniversaries. Every Sunday they spent the afternoon in their bedroom with the door locked. Sometimes we went into my brother's room and held a glass up to the wall that bordered their bedroom so that we could hear them talk and giggle. Bed springs squeaked. Eventually we tired of such things and believed that all children overheard their parents in private moments. It was a natural part of life between a man and woman.

"What's most important in life?" I said.

"A good, good friend," Lynda said.

Nora raised her glass and added, "Hear, hear." She went on, "The men come and go. A good girlfriend is there through the whole mess."

"Someone who knows everything about you and shares your view?"

Nora pushed her chair back. For a minute I thought she had lost patience with me. She groaned and shook her head.

"No, no, no. Not that. Mutual respect and trust, that's what I'm talking about—it sounds so basic, but it's rare. Too many people preach, try to give advice when it isn't solicited. And then there's the judgment."

I let it sink in. Until now, with Nora's criteria I had one such friend in my life, a woman I'd been close to in college, named Joy. Joy was arty and liberal while I was then conservative and traditional. Still, we clicked. I saw her through her parents' struggle with alcohol and abuse, and she was with me with my father died. When Joy was struggling with whether to come out of the closet, I told her she would always be the same woman to me and that I would always love her.

Joy always listened and then sometimes made me think about my opinion. My Taurus horoscope sign accurately described my stubbornness and inability to think long-term. She teased me about it without criticism. She waited, always comfortable with silence and time—I had learned so much from her and our friendship that I'd always yearned for another.

Just then Lynda glanced at me and winked. She had become my second friend. The mariachis made their way toward our table. I let the music take me away. Such heavy thoughts on a day that felt so carefree.

I slept later than normal. A whir of lawnmowers and Spanish woke me up. I rubbed my eyes after a glance at the clock: 8 a.m. Lynda had her back to me in the adjacent bed, supported by pillows between her legs and against her backside. Wind billowed in the gauze curtains. She must have opened the sliding door during the night. "It's too hot" was a common complaint of hers. I tiptoed to the bathroom.

"I hear you," she murmured.

"You looked dead."

"The back is killing me. Or, maybe it's my neck. Hard to say. It's like they have a pact against me," she said.

I stopped and sat on the edge of her bed. I patted the covers and assured her that a shower, coffee, and a little breakfast would improve her spirits.

"God, you are such a Pollyanna. You have no idea how bad this is. Maybe Nora and I can shoot across the border and find some drugs. You can buy just about anything without a prescription."

I knew I was Lynda's sounding board, that she exaggerated to make a point and get things off her chest—that she wouldn't necessarily act on her words. Sometimes I laughed, sometimes I grimaced, and sometimes I said nothing. Discussions about physical ailments were outside my abilities. If I complained about an ache when I was a kid, Dad would tell me to think about something else. His pain threshold was off the charts, as I learned much later from my mother. Still, childhood habits die hard, and eventually I had adopted his attitude.

Lynda pushed the covers back and inched her way to the edge of the bed. Her puffy eyes and disheveled hair revealed a sleepless night. The muscles along her jaw line were taut, and she moaned.

"Not good, cookie." I helped her stand as best I could. She tried to straighten up but winced. "Maybe just a little longer in bed. You could grab some Tylenol from my bag—about as useful as jello to a cancer patient."

My terror must have shown on my face. She tossed the pills in her mouth and sipped the water. She faked a smile and assured me she'd be okay in a half hour. I wanted to believe her. I decided to go for a run and give her some privacy, or maybe, give myself some space.

The morning air smelled of mesquite. I started down the hill to the main road and nodded at a hiker coming up the other way. Running had become my therapy. Some runners used the alone-time to appreciate scenery or concentrate on their running technique. I noticed the sunrise if I went out early enough, but that was about it. Instead, I focused on all I needed to accomplish over the rest of the day. When it was over,

I congratulated myself on doing something good for my body. The truth was I hated exercise but loved the result.

Lynda had physical issues, to be sure. I couldn't figure out how to be the kind of friend who could help her through the crisis. Or, worst case, aid her throughout the life changes that would leave her sedentary.

As my morning jog ended, I tried running back up the hill to the resort while I still had energy. It was a bad idea. In no time I was gasping for air and laughing at my over-confidence.

Lynda had showered and looked remarkably better. She said the Tylenol worked wonders. Even if she lied, I liked the change in her demeanor. It foretold a good day.

We met Nora in the hotel dining room for what she claimed was her second breakfast. I assumed she'd have coffee and toast, or some other light fare. She ordered up pancakes and bacon. Lynda rolled her eyes.

"What?" Nora said. "I rode Dolly out to check on a fence and then cleaned out her stall, not to mention all the other morning chores. Or maybe I just like padding your bill." She elbowed Lynda.

After a while, I asked what the plan was for the day. I wanted to see Nora's ranch, but there had been reluctance when I brought it up the day before. Maybe one of them would give me an opening to bring it up again.

"Nogales gets my vote," Lynda said, "and then tacos at Carolina's." Nora murmured agreement as she sopped up the last bite of pancake with extra syrup.

"I've never been across the border," I said. "Is it dangerous?"

They looked at me like I was an alien. I had read stories about gang shootings and drug busts. Someone at work had a friend who did something wrong in a bar and ended up in jail for over a year. He said the police there were corrupt.

"No worse than south Phoenix," Lynda said.

"What are we shopping for?" Nora said and looked around for our waitress.

"Painkillers. Powerful ones." Lynda raised her eyebrows. "I'm going to solve this problem one way or another. I'm sure Dr. Gonzalvez can fix it."

Nora's bewildered expression concerned me. All of the fun of the trip evaporated among stalled responses and uncomfortable subject matter.

"I think I'll stay here and hang out at the pool," I said.

Lynda's jaw twitched. Nora forced a nod.

By the time I organized my beach bag and got my bathing suit on, the girls had left for Nogales. I fiddled with my visor to get it tight enough without giving myself a headache and tried not to dwell on their shopping expedition. Or the border. They were accustomed to spending time in Mexico, but leaving my comfort zone in search of adventure was never my choice.

Who was Dr. Gonzalvez? His name sounded familiar—she'd talked with him before. Did he prescribe illegal drugs? I tried to take my mind off the matter with the crossword. I was angry with myself for not going with them, for being terrified of the unknown, where it was dark. The dark spooked me. When I was a kid and described the hideous things I pictured waiting for me there, Dad said I had an active imagination. Maybe so. Maybe still so.

Lynda and Nora were gone the whole afternoon. I finally returned to the room and napped. More than two hours in the Arizona sun would sap your strength.

A door slammed and woke me up. Lynda limped to my bed with Nora right behind her. I rubbed my eyes and sat up.

"Nothing," Lynda sighed. "Dr. Gonzalvez wasn't as cooperative as he used to be. Go figure. The only good thing that happened was lunch. How about you, cookie?"

I touched Lynda's arm. "What were you looking for? If you don't mind me asking."

Nora stood at the window with her hands on her hips. Either she was deep in thought or she didn't want to talk.

"I can take a lot of pain, even hard times. But, at a minimum, I need a life. Now I have no life and all the pain in the world. There's no use crying about it ... it's just the way things are," Lynda said. "A new narcotic could have given life back to me. Tennis and walking George. It would be enough."

"There's hardly anyone at the pool," Nora said. "I think a swim would help, Lynda-lou."

Lynda looked lost. I scoured my brain for the right words but I sensed her total despair. Anything I could say felt like it would be a lie. Tests and doctors' opinions had concluded that surgery held no hope. The drugs she had taken for years no longer worked, and not even cortisone gave her enough relief to justify the pain of the shot. What would become of her?

The pool soothed frayed nerves. Nora and I watched Lynda's every move, almost as if we feared she'd drown. Lynda hated pity and I knew she noticed our watchful eyes. She splashed water at both of us and made faces. "Want to race to the end of the pool?" she said to Nora.

"No contest," Nora yelled and shoved off.

Lynda gained on her. I cheered—jumping up and down and yelling. They kicked up waves and flailed through the water. For a brief moment it looked like Lynda might win but she faded quickly and lost by a body length. The two hugged briefly and had a conversation that I couldn't hear.

Soon after, Lynda hobbled behind Nora and me back to the room to get ready for our last night together. "I'm not done yet," she mumbled as we headed down the hallway. "Only the good die young, so there's hope for me."

It was a night of toasts: first for friends, then for Peter, then for all the horse adventures that Nora and Lynda had shared, then for love ... and that was about when it got melancholy. Not sad or sappy, more like a sigh that expressed the memory of a wonderful time.

"You're about to have the life you deserve," Lynda said to me. "Gary will be good for you and Robin. I am pissed that I didn't get you for my daughter-in-law but delighted for everything that's about to come your way. You are such a good girl."

Holding back tears left me spent. I didn't want to think about it. My life was full of positive energy, and Lynda deserved the same.

On the trip back to Phoenix, I concentrated on navigating through traffic to distract my thoughts. Some-time soon I would have to announce my move date, September 16. Even though it was almost two months away, it would arrive before Lynda was prepared.

"That Coleen girl said that my house will be ready in January. You think that's realistic?" she said.

"I hope Ahwatukee is ready for you. They might have to redefine 'active adult community,'" I said.

She groaned and motioned toward a truck coming up fast behind us. Backseat driving was in her blood, no matter how much I teased her about it. Once, in frustration, I'd pulled onto the shoulder and told her if she was going to continue her back-seat instruction, she should get in the back seat. She laughed and stayed put. It did make a noticeable dent in her bossy behavior but only for a week or so. When I first drove with her, I assumed she advised me because she thought my driving was bad, but after a short while, I observed that she gave advice to all, completely nondiscriminatory.

"I don't know about any new definition. How about tart-tongued? That would fit, plus I love the alliteration," she said. Her lower lip stuck out as if she were a second grader grounded from recess.

Her gloom spread throughout the car. My immediate concern was to get her home before her back and neck caused her unbearable discomfort. Staying in one position for more than an hour usually brought drastic consequences.

"C'mon. We'll think of something for your pain," I said. Talk was cheap for me.

I tried to remember the worst physical pain I had experienced: a recent toothache that led to a root canal came to mind. Breaking my wrist while roller-skating, occasional upset stomachs with vomiting, a groin muscle pulled during a marathon. Really there was nothing I remembered that was constant or debilitating. It was impossible to imagine just what she dealt with. The cortisone shot undid me because I was so afraid of needles. More than once I'd passed out just giving a blood sample.

How long has her pain been so bad?

"Can we stop somewhere? Buy something to help?" I said.

Her head stayed bowed into her chest. She didn't answer, but I knew she heard me. There was no way she could be sleeping in such a condition.

When we arrived in Tempe, I got her inside the house and settled on the couch. She moaned that she couldn't walk another step. I took her suitcase and other things into the bedroom and unpacked for her. Several bottles of prescription pills fell out of her cosmetic case. I wrapped my hand around two bottles and returned to the living room.

"Would any of these work?" I said.

Her eyes opened as I neared and bent down for her to see them. She shook her head.

"If I can be still for a couple of hours it should be better. I don't know what else to do right now," she said.

I made tea. It was worth a try, for nothing more than to make her smile at my simple remedy.

She tried to sit up, but I coaxed her back down. "It's here on the coffee table if you feel like it. I'll leave you to rest and check back later."

"Nora is something," she said before I left, "no?"

6

LIFE CHANGES

As soon as I got to my office and checked my messages, I called Lynda's son John to discuss her health. His stiffness made me want to apologize for bothering him.

"These problems with her back are nothing new. The doctors warned her long ago to quit riding due to the damage she'd done. She wasn't much for their advice and continued to ride and fall. Not even Peter could reason with her stubborn streak," John said as he let out a big breath.

"I'm so worried. She's not like her old self—she's despondent. The pain is just too much," I said.

John talked to someone in the background before returning his attention to our conversation. "Sorry, it's a zoo around my office today. I mean, what can be done? She will have to deal with it, that's all. It's not like she didn't know the risk she took way back when."

I felt more frustrated than I had before I called. Lynda and Tim shared almost everything, but I couldn't make a call to Tim, and it seemed useless to ask John to do so.

Doctors remained on a pedestal in my mind. In the past I had heeded their advice and gotten better. Others in my family had done the same. Only Dad had a problem that the best couldn't fix. The current situation made me pause to consider what fate awaited me. John's harsh stance about Lynda being warned sounded like he thought she deserved exactly what she got.

People want a certain kind of life. When health deteriorates and a new plan needs to be adopted, not everyone can do it. Dad was cautioned about manual labor and all his activity with the Percheron horses. He tried to change and couldn't. Mom told me that he said he wanted to live his life in the way he always had, even if it meant less time on the planet. Lynda, too, had made a risky choice. I doubted that she regretted any of her decisions; she wasn't the type to look over her shoulder and lament the past.

Gary and I began to work on the logistics of a fall move and wedding. It became clear that tackling both was too much. I had the condo to sell, a new job to secure, my current job to perform, and decisions to make about which items to take, since we seemed to have two of everything. The summer heat didn't help my mood or tolerance. We decided that a September move was too soon and settled on October 16, with the wedding scheduled for January 12, 1980.

I shared the dates with Lynda. Her face had a pinched look. "I'm trying to be excited and happy for you," she said. "I don't want to be remembered as the bubble pricker."

"You'll come to the wedding, of course. It's a bleak time of the year but I would love for you to be there," I said. She nodded reluctantly.

It was rare that she visited me in Phoenix, but more and more often these days, she suggested making the drive. Maybe it gave her something to do. The street where she had lived with Peter years before was on the way to my condo. I wondered if she ever checked it out but never asked.

As we sat at my kitchen table, Prince appeared and rubbed against her leg. She scratched his ears. I poured her more coffee and brought the cookie jar.

"Chocolate chip with coconut and pecans," I said.

She smacked her lips. Pain hadn't affected her sweet tooth. Maybe the worst had ebbed. I wanted to believe it, in any case.

"I can walk a little now," she said. "Not that it doesn't hurt, but I manage. George loves his walks, and it's my only exercise."

"How about the pool? That would help, no?"

"Maybe. The water does feel good. I could paddle around using the raft." She wolfed down one cookie and took another. Then, out of the blue, she asked, "What's Gary's mother like?"

I explained that Elaine had been widowed and left without life insurance at fifty-four, that she had gotten a job at a bakery, started to drive, and then balance a check book.

"Wow."

I nodded. "She's a good girl, is the best way I can describe her. All her kids love her, she doesn't interfere in any of their lives, and she's a happy person."

"She never wanted to marry again?" Lynda said.

I'd asked Gary the same question after I'd first met his family at Thanksgiving dinner, so now I repeated to Lynda what he'd told me: "Apparently an old boyfriend reappeared after her husband passed away and wanted to revitalize whatever they had. Two of the kids met the guy and liked him, plus they said he was rich. She decided after one dinner date that she wasn't interested. She likes living alone."

Lynda stood up and arched her back. She put the cookie jar away, saying it was too tempting. "You know, Nancy, there is freedom in being alone. I didn't think I would ever say I prefer it, but I know how Elaine feels."

I made a circle with my index finger on the table top—as if I were gathering up dust. "You're never scared or lonely?" She scowled at me as if I had just asked the dumbest question in the world and motioned for me to put Prince in her lap. Bending over had become painful for her.

Prince rested his head on her arm, twitching his tail back and forth. The cat could go to sleep in record time.

"I predict that it will be the best of the best for you, dahling. Will there be a church wedding?" she giggled a little.

"Something simple, just family in our house—maybe a reception afterwards for all the friends. We really haven't made any plans, not to mention that we don't even have the house yet. I tend to get ahead of myself."

Lynda delighted at the news of a visit from Robin over Labor Day. It would be the last one before my move to Seattle. Ever since Robin's first visit, it had been Lynda who scoured the newspaper for things to do with kids. Maybe she solicited advice from neighbors or was just more diligent than I in reading up on trends, but I came to rely on her research and flare for surprise. Robin learned quickly that Lynda was the social director, and her first question was always, "What did Lynda pick for us to do?"

This time, we headed over to Phoenix's Wet 'n' Wild Park. Labor Day was the last weekend in the year it would be open. A huge man-made wave plummeted kids on rafts, and without rafts, onto a beach of sorts. Robin coaxed me to try it with her. It was scarier than I'd thought it would be. I landed headlong into brown, gritty sand that coursed its way into every part of my suit. Robin laughed hysterically. Afterward, I retreated under a beach umbrella with Lynda. Shrieks of joy wafted over from a giant slide that corkscrewed into deep water. An occasional parent braved the slide, providing entertainment for us. For a while, I thought we'd never leave and prayed Robin couldn't sense my boredom.

Lynda picked Farrell's Ice Cream Parlour for lunch, another special treat. We ordered small sandwiches so that we'd have room for the banana split trough, which two waiters delivered with elaborate fanfare. Even though three of us shared the extravagance, we never came close to finishing it. I thought I'd burst, but Lynda and Robin agreed it was just enough.

"We should have asked for a doggie bag," Lynda said as we headed toward our car. Robin laughed and made a face. She told Lynda how silly that was.

"Swimming pool, swimming pool," Robin said. She skipped alongside Lynda and grabbed her hand. "I like you."

The spontaneous remark was so pure and sweet, I felt my heart in my throat. I glanced at Lynda to see if it had affected her. "And I like you too," she said. Either it didn't have the impact it did on me, or she covered it up. Robin was my kid—I reacted differently to her words.

"Should we go shopping for school clothes or do you still want the swimming pool?" Lynda said.

Robin stopped and rubbed her chin. "I don't want to pick one. Can we do both?"

Lynda nodded to me. "She is your daughter."

"How come you're walking funny?" Robin said.

I started to answer for Lynda because she hesitated. Robin looked at me, confused, as if there were a secret. Lynda held up her hand.

"Old injuries are coming back to haunt me," she finally said. Robin pressed for details.

"I rode horses for years and fell a lot," Lynda said. "When you're young, sometimes you can overcome such things. Other times, as you get older, you have to pay the price."

Robin stroked her hand in sympathy. "That's terrible. It hurts to walk?"

It had been a full day for everyone. After Robin and I left Lynda, all I wanted was a shower and a glass of wine. Robin helped me prepare extra toppings for the pizza. Prince curled up on the dining room floor and raised his head every so often so as not to miss it if we dropped a piece of cheese or sausage.

"Mom, will Lynda be okay?" Robin asked.

How to answer?

"She has pain most of the time. Right now there isn't much the doctors can do to fix it. Some days are better than others. There is medicine that helps a little," I said.

Robin didn't seem to hear me. She had moved to the cat and was playing with him as I talked. Maybe it was better that way. I didn't know how much to say, how truthful to be.

As with all of Robin's visits to Arizona, the time ended prematurely. I fooled myself into thinking that I would not be sad if I could add just one more day. When the good times were over, they were over. Goodbyes left me empty.

"Are you sad, Mommy?" Robin asked as we drove to the airport. I shook my head, trying to convince her. I needed to be strong.

"Next time I see you it will be in Seattle. Thanksgiving," I said.

She pouted. "Rain, rain, rain. That's what Dad said."

"It will be different, but you'll like it."

"But what about Prince?" she said. "He's lived in the desert all his life."

We laughed about all the new things Prince would see in Seattle. He'd never seen a squirrel or been near water. The house that Gary and I had our eyes on had a large wooded lot directly across the street from Lake Sammamish, a work of nature that measured one mile wide and twelve miles long. Fifty shades of green and other lush vegetation framed it. That would be some different territory for the cat.

"I'll see you in two months," I repeated as I hugged Robin goodbye at the gate. She marched toward the stewardess who escorted her onto the plane. One last wave and then she was out of sight.

Sunshine nearly blinded me as I made my way out of the terminal. My eyes watered. The kid had flourished with Sam in the lead. She was a model of well-adjusted behavior. The sacrifice I'd made when I'd left her with him seemed insignificant in the bigger picture—she didn't remember her parental situation any other way. My heart ached for all the things I was missing in her childhood. *For a girl who hates to cry, I sure am doing a lot of it.*

As with all my sad times, I threw myself into work. After a hard day's work I could be rational, or maybe too tired to cry. I needed to accept that though I would miss the day-to-day of Robin's childhood, at least Sam and I didn't fight over her. We appreciated each other's contribution to her happiness. More and more, I reminded myself of that.

As for my friendship with Lynda, she and I enjoyed our time together and helped each other. Nothing would change, I told myself. I wanted to believe that we would replace our daily interaction with some other form of communication once I moved to Seattle.

The change would be hard, I knew it. I tried to analyze my sadness as if it were a work problem, but job issues were easy compared to emotional ones. I had been accused at times of being cold and callous because of the way I covered up my feelings. The behavior had to go back to my early years, to Dad's distaste for tears. Unlike Dad, though, I didn't hate them on other people, only on myself.

I let Lynda plan our last week together. She scheduled something different for each day, an activity that related to our past. I grumbled when she told me that we were having lunch at La Petite Maison, the place where we'd met Jean Claude. She assured me he no longer worked there, but I caught her sly smile and could only hope she told the truth.

After we were seated I smiled at her. "What did I do for a friend before you?"

She leaned forward. "Those were dark years."

Before we left the restaurant, she pulled a box out of her Goldwater's department store shopping bag. There were bold black letters across the top—SEATTLE SURVIVAL KIT—and underneath, a big red cross, like the American Red Cross logo.

I giggled. "You are such a kick. How do you come up with these ideas?"

She shrugged and motioned for me to open the box. Inside, were a fold-up umbrella, two pairs of tiny boots for Prince (hilarious), a cookbook featuring twenty ways to prepare salmon, a shower cap, a map of the state of Washington, a pair of wool socks, a box of tea bags, and stamps. I pondered on the stamps until she said that she expected to hear from me once a week. I laughed.

"No, I'm not kidding, cookie," she said.

We took our time walking to the car. She sighed and said how different the coming Thanksgiving would be.

"You'll come to Seattle. It's perfect," I said. "You can see the place for yourself and meet Gary's family."

It was the biggest smile I'd seen on her face in weeks. She accepted. I suddenly hoped it would be okay with Gary. I knew that Robin would be delighted.

Gary arrived in Phoenix and insisted on taking Lynda out the night before the move. Over dinner, he sensed my nervousness and joked, but conversation didn't flow and the silence was uncomfortable. Lynda hardly touched her prime rib, a sure sign that the evening was a bust.

The three of us stood outside her house. Lynda hugged Gary first and then turned to me. "A new adventure is right in front of you, Nancy.

Be happy," she said and leaned in to kiss my cheek. "Don't let the rain ruin your parade."

She limped slightly through the gate. I backed up toward the car but watched her the whole way. She unlocked the front door without looking back at me. I waved just in case.

Gary and I sat in the driveway for several seconds. He started the car and turned to me. "You okay?" It was hard to explain how I felt. Maybe I didn't know, myself; maybe it was too hard to interpret. Women connect differently.

The drive to Seattle started in ninety-five-degree weather on October 16, 1979. By day two, in northern California, shorts and a tee shirt no longer cut it. The temperature was in the fifties in the early morning. By the time we hit the mountain pass between California and Oregon, there was snow. The Monte Carlo skidded on occasion, and I gripped the armrest.

"It's unusual to see snow and ice this time of year," Gary said as he drove. A lack of experience made it impossible for me to comment. I pulled sweats over my insufficient clothing and tried to be positive. Prince whined in his carrier from the backseat but eventually quieted when no one paid any attention.

"How much farther is it?" I tried to make it sound like an innocent question instead of a complaint. Car travel had never been my favorite. It took forever, and I felt like a caged animal with nothing to do except listen to the radio. Reading was impossible because I would get carsick. I'd grow bored and then I'd become Queen Crabby. No matter what I had tried, the outcome remained the same. When Gary said it would be at least ten more hours, I scowled. He thought I was being funny.

He'll learn this is no joke soon enough.

I thought the drive couldn't get worse, but sixty miles into Oregon, the rain started, gently at first. I gazed out the window and saw ten shades of gray and black clouds. I thought of the sunshine and warmth I had left behind, and my mood went from worse to suicidal.

Gary glanced over at me. "It takes a while to get used to."

"How much does it rain? Really?" I said.

He looked in the rearview mirror and put on the turn signal to pass a slow driver in front of us.

"It depends. Winter is the worst. Summer is nice—hardly rains at all in August."

I laughed. He could spin anything in a positive light.

"Keep in mind how much you love all the green," he added. "It wouldn't be that way without rain."

I snuggled into my seat and closed my eyes. There was a lot to look forward to I reminded myself. Gary had bought the house that we both had wanted, the one with the view of Lake Sammamish, amidst tall pines and wild vegetation. I hadn't seen it since the sale had closed, but Gary had moved in. We'd finally decided that my antiques and few rugs would blend our households together, and I had shipped them the week before. I tried to visualize the four stories of cedar and glass. Almost no one had a two-story or a contemporary house in Arizona, let alone all of the stairs I'd soon be climbing. The difference excited me, even if I thought I might have gray hair by the time we arrived.

New job, new house, new city, life with a new man ... it was enough to take me off the charts, stress-wise. Lynda claimed the more I had on my plate the better I liked it. I wasn't so sure. Some say stress from a move is right behind stress from the death of a loved one.

Gary was a Gemini and true to the twin sign. In a crowd, he met people and talked easily, social and outgoing like the salesman that he was. Once out of the group, he hunkered down and quieted in the way of someone who likes being in his own skin and alone. He never got upset, didn't seem to worry. He could be the most laid back businessman I had ever known.

My thoughts drifted to Lynda. She'd become a clerk at Bloomingdale's right out of high school. It was hard to believe that anyone could handle such a job at eighteen. I pictured her with smiling eyes and a strong chin, giving advice to a customer, or telling someone that what she had picked out didn't highlight her features in the best way. She had diplomacy but also confidence in her own opinion. Tim had often said that she was seldom right but never in doubt, which made me laugh.

Sometimes her pushiness angered me, but I had learned, finally, not to ask her viewpoint if I didn't want the truth.

Gary wasn't as blunt and outspoken as Lynda was. There had been lots of drama with Lynda, and at the time, I'd loved it. My new relationship would require an adjustment. As the miles clicked on toward Seattle, some kind of peace fell over me. It was time for change.

When we got to our new house on the third day, I came alive, despite the persistent rain. Gary got a fire going in the living room and Prince sprinted up the stairs to survey his new home. The floor-to-ceiling windows on either side of the fireplace let in plenty of light along with the view of Lake Sammamish. I sat on the couch and spread my legs out. There was so much about the house that I had forgotten. It was like unwrapping a gift. Our house had drama, if not size. There were two bedrooms, each with a sleeping loft. The bed in the spare room was accessible by ladder, while the master had stairs. For a split second I considered that it might be hard to sell some day just because the arrangement was so unusual. The four levels of living space added up to only 2,200 square feet, with stairs at every turn.

"I can't imagine Lynda climbing that ladder," I mumbled. Gary stoked the fire. He rubbed his chin, considering the problem.

"We could put two beds in that room, one in the loft and one on the main floor," he said. "How about that?" It was the perfect solution. A year later, Lynda would entertain us with a story about how Prince had learned to climb the ladder and then jump from the loft onto the bed below, like a kid would do. Only Lynda was asleep in the lower level and it was the middle of the night.

The next month Lynda came for Thanksgiving. I couldn't wait to see her and share my adjustments much more honestly than I had done up to then. Lynda and I talked at least twice a week, but I never spoke truthfully. I didn't want to reveal how hard my transition was, and I suspected she had masked her health issues as well. We usually ended up discussing some current event, a movie, or some antic of Prince's. Gary had been attentive and helpful, but I couldn't share the pain of my loneliness with him. My new job in downtown Seattle had been especially difficult to get used to. I didn't like selling copy services instead of equipment, I had made only one friend, the weather had remained dreary, and my daily trials of getting lost in the city hadn't lessened. I knew that, in person, Lynda would provide a sympathetic ear and find humor in all of it. "You do have a good guy," was something I knew she'd point out, and I agreed. My new guy wasn't the problem.

Gary's mother Elaine hosted the turkey day and was anxious to meet our houseguest. On the forty-mile drive, Gary amused us with stories of his Tacoma childhood. He remembered that all the kids had wanted their Mom to sell their brick ranch house after their dad died. They'd assumed it would require too much upkeep.

"Some women stay put for the memories," Lynda said.

Lynda presented Elaine with a holiday plant and two bottles of wine. The two hugged briefly before Lynda glimpsed the lavish display spread on the sideboard.

"You made all this and dinner too?" Lynda said. Elaine nodded, her shoulders rolled inward with her hands in apron pockets like it was nothing. I assumed that she'd made a production because of two extra guests—Lynda and me—but Gary's siblings said she did the same thing every year regardless of who was coming. Appetizers of Swedish meatballs, deviled eggs, a cheese ball rolled in pecans with Ritz crackers, tiny rolls of prosciutto ham around melon slices, and vegetables with dip.

"We may have to spend the night to get through all this," Lynda said.

After dinner, Lynda and Gary's sister Marianne cleaned up the mess while the rest of us huddled around a football game on TV, and though it seemed strange, the conversation turned to baseball. The boys liked to discuss baseball with Elaine because she kept up on all the stats, trades, and what might be in store for the spring. It amazed me how much Elaine knew about the players and the history. Her voice became vibrant and she expressed herself with her hands. I had never known a woman who cared so much about a game I found boring beyond description.

"How did you become so fascinated with baseball?" I said when there was a lull in the conversation.

Her eyebrows furrowed. She grunted like I had asked a stupid question but then smiled at me. She was too nice a person to make me uncomfortable.

"I played," she said matter-of-factly.

Elaine stood about 5'2" and probably weighed 170 pounds. This was no longer the body of an athlete.

"What position did you play?" Lynda said, coming in from the kitchen. She would later admit that she knew I was tongue-tied and needed to be saved.

When Elaine answered catcher, another shock wave hit me. I just couldn't picture it. She dug through a side table drawer and pulled out a yellowed photo of teenage girls in baseball uniforms.

"That's me," she said to Lynda and pointed to a girl sitting cross-legged in the front row. Lynda smiled and passed the photo to me.

"I am impressed, Elaine. That could never have been me because I have always been afraid of the ball," I said, deciding to share an embarrassing bit of truth about myself to bridge the awkward silence.

Elaine, Gary, and his brothers chuckled. They probably thought I was making it up, but I wasn't. Since childhood anything that involved speed terrified me. Riding a bicycle at full tilt gave me goose bumps in the same way that a roller coaster did.

I remembered a time that Lynda had hit a tennis ball right at my head and I'd ducked instead of trying to hit it. She had howled. I hoped she wouldn't share that story. Before that could happen, the boys took the pressure off by asking Elaine to reminisce about her team days. She delighted in sharing stories.

Can't tell a book by its cover.

"That's how I met Bud," Elaine was saying, referring to her late husband. "He came to see us play with a bunch of his friends. They didn't think girls could play baseball."

"And you won him over with your prowess," Lynda smiled.

Elaine's face reddened for a moment. "Catcher is a hard position. There's a lot going on all the time. You are in a crouched position for most of the game and you need eyes in the back of your head."

"Which was perfect training to be mother to five kids," Gary said. "We could never get away with a thing." All the siblings nodded.

"Tell Lynda and Nancy about the singing," Marianne said.

Elaine looked flustered, but she explained. "Sometimes they asked me to sing the national anthem, I never thought I was any good, but I would do it if they needed me. Fifteen years ago someone who had heard me put in a good word, and I got to sing on *Lawrence Welk.*"

Lynda and I raved. Again, I was surprised and delighted by this modest and understated talent. I looked over at Gary who had one arm draped over Elaine's shoulders.

"That's my momma," he said.

"Enough about me," Elaine said. "It was a long time ago."

Lynda didn't argue when I climbed into the back seat for the ride home. It had been a lot of conversation, pressing the flesh with new people, too much food, and a lack of quiet time. I felt undone.

"Your family discusses everything so openly," Lynda said. "It's refreshing to see no family tension or behind-the-back stuff." Gary smiled.

"I think it's unusual," she said. I thought the same thing.

"Well, as open as we are, it surprised me that no one asked about the wedding," Gary said. The family knew the date and that instead of a formal church affair, we planned a small ceremony in our house with a party for family and friends afterward. Maybe Elaine didn't think much of that, or maybe weddings didn't concern her. She did seem to roll with things.

"Elaine said she was looking forward to meeting her new grand-daughter at Christmas, so indirectly that's a comment about the wedding," I said.

"I didn't hear that," Gary said.

"And when she hugged me good-bye," I paused, "she whispered in my ear that she was very happy for us."

Lynda stayed with us for five days. I took her to the Space Needle and Pike's Place Market. She marveled at the fish salesmen who threw salmon around for entertainment. I knew she was a water person and would love the ferry ride to Bainbridge Island, where we could have lunch. She and I stood on the deck for the thirty-minute ride and took in the view of downtown Seattle and the small island town as we approached.

"How romantic it would be to live on the island and commute to Seattle," she said. I nodded without enthusiasm. She linked her arm in mine.

"It'll take some time, cookie," she said. Tears streamed down my cheeks.

"I had no idea how much I was turning my world upside down," I said, barely aloud.

Lynda stared at the island dock as we neared.

"One day at a time. Tackle one problem at a time," she said and squeezed my arm. "Hey, if you hate the job find another. Work is a big part of your life; don't stay in something you hate."

A sliver of sunshine perked me up. She was so intuitive about my issues. Suddenly everything seemed easier.

"You are so smart," I said.

"Damn straight," she said. "Now, where on this gorgeous island are we planning to have lunch? All this cool weather has given me an appetite."

Lynda took in all the sights with glee. She said it was a true vacation with nothing about the terrain or weather similar to home. She had brought two pairs of shorts—even though she had been to Seattle when she was younger, somehow she hadn't been able to imagine that she wouldn't need them.

"It is just a split second from winter now," I said. "They say that shorts might be dusted off for an hour in August."

During lunch, Lynda pulled out a prescription bottle and took out three pills. I gave her a "what gives?" look.

"New drug. Stronger but I'm quickly needing more to do the trick," she said. "What I have to take in order to just walk around a little and take George for a stroll."

I leaned in. "I'm so sorry. You looked better."

"Forget about it, although it is nice to know I look better," she laughed. "We'll see how long this one lasts. I really don't want to talk about it anymore, though. It's not the way I want to spend my time with you."

As happy as I was to see Lynda and as much as she boosted my morale, five days was too long to have a houseguest, especially one who loved to talk. Gary and I went to bed at eight the day Lynda left.

"She depends on you a lot," he said. I rolled over and faced him. We didn't discuss it further. Her health had transformed the way she lived from day to day. There had always been something I could recommend, some advice I could give her that worked, but that also had come to an abrupt ending. I was fresh out of ideas.

In my life, whenever a problem came up, my instinct was either to solve it or ignore it completely. I had never been much of a worry-wart. That fall, I tried to control my anxiety by focusing, as Lynda had suggested, on one thing at a time. Christmas and Robin's first visit to Seattle were on the horizon, and shortly after that the wedding. Then there was the job situation. The new way of approaching customers and the different selling strategy were so foreign that I struggled with the changes. Some nights I was in tears privately, fraught with failure. For the first time business did not come easily.

One particular morning on the commute into Seattle, I made a u-turn and returned home, sobbing the whole way. It might have been a pity party or it could have been a melt-down from having too much on my plate. Robin had not wanted me to leave Arizona, and then there was Lynda. I cried on and off most of the morning. I wondered if I had done the right thing. A trail of used Kleenex littered the house. Prince followed me from room to room. Whenever I paused and fell into a chair he leaped into my lap and peered up at me. I stroked him. His gorgeous face made me smile.

"If I just had one girlfriend to talk to," I said. Finally I pulled myself together and started back into town and work. On the way, I decided to lower the bar. Come up with a plan for a small victory each day. There really wasn't anyone who could do it for me, not even Gary. Especially not Gary. Love had blinded me to all the adjustments I would have to make, not to mention the depressing weather. I noticed that people in the northwest seemed to accept the weather by giving a sunny day special attention and appreciation. Someone reminded me of the Perry Como song about how the bluest skies in all the land were in Seattle, and true enough, when it was sunny there was no prettier place.

Lynda had said that the gray, cool, Seattle weather invigorated her. She claimed it hydrated her skin. Quite possibly she wanted to make me feel better about the move and my future. She was smart that way and often knew me better than I knew myself.

Slowly I began to see positive aspects of life in the northwest that hadn't been part of life in the southwest. Serious outdoor adventure was the norm, as was a wonderful respect for nature and its preservation, a deep reserve of capital, an open business environment for minorities and women, and less of an interest in the display of material wealth. All of those things appealed to me. At the time, residential real estate values lined up with costs in Arizona, which stunned me. Seattle neighborhoods had more charm and variation.

At home, we were settling in, working on using all of the four stories of our house. The first floor, more of a daylight basement, had a pool table and outdoor hot tub. This delighted Robin, who became a pool shark extraordinaire. As much as I fretted over the loft guest bedroom, she loved the idea of climbing the ladder to her bed with the globe window. Nothing about the house was like the home she lived in with Sam in Akron or my ranch house in Arizona. She tromped through the woods next door with Prince and looked forward to the summer months, when we planned to go to the park for picnics and swimming in Lake Sammamish.

Two weeks after Christmas and during the worst snowstorm in decades, Gary and I stood in front of our fireplace to exchange our wedding vows. My mother, Lynda, and Gary's family were the only ones able to attend. Because of inopportune vacation schedule, Robin could not attend. We wrote our own vows, replacing "until death do us part" with "friends until the end." Everyone thought we were very modern, including the justice of the peace. Prince showed up near the end and stood next to Gary, his new best friend. A few people giggled.

"What a great day this is," Gary said and then kissed me long.

Once we got to the reception, by way of heavy-duty vehicles equipped with snow tires and chains, the weather was forgotten. Forty or so friends joined our families for the celebration. A few people were confused about the presence of three mothers, but Lynda took care of that, disclosing her almost-mother title. I worried for a minute that she'd elaborate, explaining how we'd met, but it wasn't necessary. No one asked for more detail.

Mom and Lynda took the two beds in the spare room. We heard laughter and talking late into all three nights of their stay. Their connection pleased me. I had so much support from Elaine, Lynda, and Mom that I slowly quit thinking about my problems and accepted how fortunate I was.

Even though I was able to adjust on several fronts over the next year, my job never improved. Selling services required much more cold-calling as well as communicating with several people within each company. My previous training had been to approach one person about buying a copy machine, usually the company's office manager. Machines were bigger-ticket items than a simple copy job or a one-time special project. As much as I tried to change my attitude, my heart wasn't in it. I knew I was on the verge of getting fired.

"You're thirty-four years old," Lynda said. "I think it's okay if you finally fail at something."

I twisted the phone cord around my finger as I sat in the conference room and listened to her. All of the pressure left my body. I smiled, even. I wanted to do something else. Commercial real estate had my eye. Interest rates were eighteen percent in 1981 and although some questioned my judgment, I reasoned that getting into the business when things were bad was a good time to do it—things could only go up. I wanted to be a part of something bigger than copy services and machines.

"I think you'd do very well in commercial real estate," Gary said before I had finished my pitch on why I wanted out of Xerox.

Lynda never said anything negative about the plans I had for myself. Her enthusiastic response to my schemes always gave me strength. She loved to hear about the obstacles I encountered and how I planned to overcome them. Sometimes she had good ideas, too—it was still evident why she'd been successful at Bloomingdale's. In fact, she had so much moxie that I suggested she get a job. I reasoned that it would take her mind off her pain and give her new goals. She laughed, apparently thinking I was kidding.

"I'd rather live through you, cookie," she said.

I shared the complexities of real estate with her and the names of the players. She was the only one who wanted to hear it all—the conversations, what I wore, how I got appointments, how I closed a deal. Possibly she took notes because she remembered names and details and asked for updates. We had never talked so much about my work in the past. Gary's only complaint was the increase in long distance phone charges.

"It's a small price to pay so that you don't have to listen to all of the drama," I said. "But you know, I can involve you in all I'm learning."

He shook his head and laughed. "You are so right: small price. I mean, I support you one thousand percent, but I don't want to hear about every detail the way she does. I don't even like to talk about my own job."

Lynda visited me twice during the first year in Seattle but I did not return to Arizona for some time. She didn't whine about my lack of trips to Phoenix or ask when I'd be back. That surprised me, considering that she was getting ready to move to Ahwatukee and transition into her new life.

Meanwhile, there had been so many delays in construction, she said the house might never be finished. I wondered if the construction crew was getting back at her for her constant supervision and advice. It had to be irritating. I gently suggested that she limit her inspections to once a week, but she would have none of that.

"Those guys never look at the plans, I swear," she said.

"Maybe they would if you weren't there."

Eventually, though, the construction entered into its final stages.

Lynda waited until the month before her new home was completed to put her villa on the market. It sold in two days for the full asking price. She bitched. What if her house was delayed again? What if she couldn't pack in time?

"Not a problem," I said. "Close the sale and lease it back. One less thing to worry about. You should be happy."

She sighed. "Okay. That's a good idea. What a smart girl you are."

Gary was bored with the situation before I finished the story. He maintained that as much as he liked Lynda, she'd never be satisfied. He didn't know whether she expected too much or if she was simply unhappy.

"Maybe she needs to have a man in her life," I said.

Gary shook his head. "That ain't gonna happen. She's got so much baggage she needs a porter."

I laughed. How much I wanted to share the joke with Lynda! But it was too much on point, and very possibly it wouldn't be funny to her.

The amount of mail from Lynda increased as she ferreted out funnier and funnier cards. She found ones that commented on grumpy moods, incompetent contractors, rainy days—all keepers. "I make the round of five stores every couple of weeks," she said. If it wasn't a card or a letter it was a gift. Something she thought I had to have and she got my tastes right every single time.

A bodysuit-style blouse that stayed tucked in came one week. The next time it was a watch that had four differently colored leather bands—it felt like perpetual Christmas, or my birthday. I wanted to do the same for her, but it was impossible. She had unpredictable tastes, whereas I was an open book. She spent as if she had unlimited funds, whereas I was careful with my money. She had the time to hunt for the perfect whatever, whereas I worked and had to devote time to my relationships with Gary and Robin. There was always something.

Finally, the construction team put the finishing touches on Lynda's house, and she moved in. She began decorating, rethinking paint colors, figuring out picture arrangements, and deciding what to do with her mini outdoor patio. Still, she didn't ask me to come back to Arizona to help.

I decided to surprise her. Reluctantly, I phoned John: I needed to make sure that she would be in town. When he said how good it was to hear from me, I nearly fainted. He didn't hurry to end the conversation and even offered to pick me up at the airport. "Lynda will be thrilled. She misses you terribly," he said.

His interest in talking made me think that they must be communicating more often. How else would he know her thoughts?

"How is her health?" I said.

He hesitated. "I believe that she has adjusted to an exercise regime of walking. She says that she doesn't miss tennis all that much. She does complain about gaining weight."

"And the pain? How is that?"

Again, he paused. "Every once in a while I ask her about it and she always changes the subject. I don't know."

I remembered that Lynda had once joked about John's conservative appearance: his short hair, clean-cut, boring clothes. "A true Boy Scout," she had said.

"Eagle Scout," John had corrected her, and then smiled a little.

After a few minutes our conversation reverted to stops and awkward starts. We finished up our talk by deciding where to meet at the airport.

Lynda had never liked surprises. She mentioned it often, each time with more force. I found it fascinating since I loved surprises. It wasn't often that someone could pull one off on me because I was such a snoop. I, however, had surprised many people over the years. On the ride from the airport, I worried. Gary told me not to think a second about it. "She'll be so happy to see you that it just won't matter," he had said.

The thirty-minute car ride with John challenged me. All his talking on the phone must have exhausted him because he didn't initiate any conversation.

Grinding out tax forms in solitude must be orgasmic.

After a couple of attempts, I decided to let him talk if he wanted and glanced out the window, feigning interest in the scenery. My pulse raced as we neared Ahwatukee. I began to chastise myself, silently, for not letting Lynda know my plan. It then occurred to me that she might be as surprised to see John as much as me. We passed house after house, crammed in so tight you could literally touch your neighbor. I sighed and mentioned this to John.

"I know what you mean," was all he said.

John carried my bag to the front door and we rang the bell.

"This should be entertaining," he said with a sly smile.

"I'm coming, I'm coming," Lynda yelled from inside. A crazed dog barked and barked. The door flew open. She stood with her hair pulled back in a bandana, a mop in her rubber-gloved hands.

"Oh my god. Oh my god! Nancy love!" she grabbed me in a fierce bear hug. "What in the world? And John, you were in on this?"

We laughed and followed her into the house. Furniture was moved off to the side and a vacuum stood in the center of the room. Cleaning products, paper towels, a bucket full of rags, a feather duster, and scrub brushes were close by. She noticed how chaotic it must look.

"This can all go away in ten minutes," she said. "There will always be time to clean. Give me just a second and we'll go out to lunch." John explained that he had to get back to work as I moseyed around and checked out the house. Unlike the development, I liked the openness and pale yellow walls inside. Some rooms were settled while others were piled with moving boxes. Helping her unpack and arrange the house would be fun.

Lynda saw John to the door and then jumped up and down, as much as she could. "I can't believe that you are here. What a great surprise. The best ever."

George stood at her side and wagged his tail, not knowing which of us deserved his attention. He seemed to remember me, but he was the kind of dog who would go to anyone after a minute or two.

"Everything is coming together in your new place," I said.

Lynda waved her hand as if she disagreed. "There is still so much to do, and I can't seem to make up my mind on where to put what."

"It seems bigger than the villa, I guess because it's so open."

She nodded. "A new concept—they call it the 'great room.' Makes sense, really. Who cares about a formal living room anymore?"

As soon as I got the leash from the drawer, George elected me his new best friend. I told Lynda I would take him for a long walk while she showered and dressed. German shepherds can walk for miles. I guessed that his exercise had been limited to strolling around the block. I walked fast to test his endurance and then escalated to a slow run. He stayed at my side. We detoured down every street before returning. Construction was underway all over. It felt denser than I had imagined it could be. George didn't mind. He eyed every worker without losing a step. Lynda trained him to stay on the left side and he obeyed. Guiding him across streets or to turn a different direction was easy. We stayed out for an hour, so long that my shins began to ache. For a minute, I worried about how to get back to Lynda's as all of the houses looked identically ugly, but George picked up the pace when we rounded a corner and led the way back home.

The woman who had bought Lynda's villa just had to have some of the furniture. I worried when I heard that because I thought her things worked in an eclectic way and showed her personality. I would have kept all of them, at least until I moved and figured out what I needed in the new place.

"I decorated the villa to be in sync with the architecture, but Ahwatukee has more of a contemporary feel," Lynda said. "It needs to be done differently, and some of my things just wouldn't work."

She had described rooms in such detail over the phone that it surprised me to see piles of boxes neatly stacked but unpacked. She caught me staring.

"Sometimes it is all I can do to get through the day. The pain is ongoing."

I smiled and gave her hug. "Lucky for you, I am an expert unpacker. I only break a few things every hour."

The dirt backyard was a fraction of the size of the yard at the villa. A tiny concrete covered patio allowed room for a small table and two chairs. Her hanging rattan chair was suspended from a beam in the opposite corner. She loved to nestle into it and swing back and forth. She called it her cocoon.

Beyond the backyard was the only green—the golf course—and way off in the distance, mountains. I remembered that Lynda said she liked the idea of desert landscaping. Maybe with enough pots, flowering shrubs and mesquite trees, the grounds would improve, but how long would that take? I could not picture it.

"At least the golf course is pretty," Lynda said. She toweled her wet hair and stood beside me. "I finally picked a landscaper I can work with to tackle this postage stamp. You wouldn't believe how much money it's going to cost." She laughed and then shook her head. "Actually, I'm sure you could believe how much."

She described Saltillo tile over the patio that would extend into the dirt area, mounded dirt and boulders with river rock to tie it together, flower pots everywhere, sawgrass, a few agave and yucca cacti along with two mesquite trees. The landscaping would improve things.

We wasted no time getting to work on rearranging furniture and writing out a shopping list of needed accessories: more pictures, an oversized mirror, throw pillows, and plants. It was like the old days.

"Some accent color could be nice on the wall across from the sofa," I said.

She took a seat and looked up and down. "Like what color? I just paid a fortune for this custom yellow shade. Wouldn't you know, it's your first idea."

"Just one wall—you'll get used to the purple," I said. We both laughed before I stood back and surveyed the whole room along with some of the furniture we'd placed.

"A rich tan, not too much contrast from the yellow," I continued. "Just enough to give it some punch."

Two days passed without any mention of her health. Each morning she stretched out on the carpet and did gentle exercises for fifteen minutes, often with great sighing and whining. Sometimes she repeated the stretches after breaking for a cup of coffee. She methodically counted each repetition out loud. Her flushed face and taut jaw told how painful it must be. I hoped that the stretches would improve her flexibility and relieve the stress on her spine.

"How is your back?" I finally asked.

"It's still crooked," she said and tried to smile. "I can stand it for a while longer."

A chill slid down my spine. I wanted to ask what she meant by that, but I didn't.

By the end of the fourth day, we'd finished all of the things on her to-do list and were sitting with a glass of iced tea, taking stock of our accomplishments. Somehow, together, we had created a charming retreat. The plants were the icing. She had wanted silk plants because she thought they would be easier. I argued that real made a huge difference—and if she killed them, so be it. Buy replacements. We picked out bromeliads, ferns, and a beautifully shaped ficus tree. We chose colorful pottery for the tree and unusual baskets for the other plants. A new furniture arrangement along with three fabulous oil paintings pulled it all together.

"You were right, cookie," Lynda said. "Real makes it work. I bet I can even keep these plants alive."

She refilled our glasses.

"It looks fabulous. You need to show off, maybe have a little cocktail party for your neighbors," I said.

Her brow furrowed. "I don't have anything in common with these people. You'd understand if you met them. I'll just enjoy being here with George."

Not what I wanted to hear but what I feared. Before I could question her further, she changed the subject. She wanted to hear the news about Gary's family. What was up with his brother, Duane, and the job at Weyerhaeuser? Was Marianne going to start a family? What about Elaine and her job at the bakery? Lynda wore me out with questions.

The detail she remembered stunned me. Sometimes I had to stop and think whether I even knew the answer. She seemed more in tune with my new family than I was.

Our ride to the airport was strained as usual by silence. Neither of us ever knew what to say when it was time to say good-bye. Our mutual inability to go deep into the emotional well probably sprung from our fear that we would lose control and not be able to get back out.

So strange that this is when we make small talk.

I figured that it would be a while until I saw her again. I gazed out the window without seeing a thing. In Seattle, I was overwhelmed with the amount of technical data I needed to learn and the number of property owners I needed to contact to make a dent in my new career in commercial real estate. It required more than ten hours a day, but I was energized in a way I had never been before. No one, except Gary and Lynda, believed I'd be successful.

"How long do you think it will take before you can exhale?" Lynda said.

She made connections like that so often—somehow picking up on my thoughts. I kidded her once that she should take up wizardry. She countered that she already had.

"I am planning on three years before I can take a breath and five to establish a solid reputation," I said. I didn't mention that the only way I got through the tough days was to practice my Broker of the Year Award acceptance speech. A silly way to do an affirmation, but it worked for me.

She whistled. "Wow. Long time."

"Compared to what?" I said.

We turned in to Sky Harbor airport and headed to the departure drop-off. She nodded. "You're right. It's a drop in the bucket compared to how long you'll be around."

On the plane, I stared out the window at Phoenix below. The sprawl for which Phoenix had come to be dubbed a mini-L.A. would probably continue to grow. Construction soaked up empty land for miles in every direction. So much had happened to me there. In a way, I'd grown up, become my own person, and made a new life. For a long time I had doubted I'd find happiness and fulfillment, but it had worked out—every year an improvement over the one before. I swallowed hard, and a tear trickled down my cheek. Like a snake that molts each year, I had shed another layer but not without pain.

My thoughts turned to Lynda. She had changed in the past two years, and I didn't know if it was just her health. She seemed to have lost the desire to fight, to try to fix the problems. It was harder to make her laugh, her caustic observations had ceased, and she didn't plan for future events. Her life bored her, she'd said, so just imagine how it must appear to others. Maybe things were worse than she told me. Maybe it was that bad. Maybe it was futile.

Emotional exhaustion took over. A headache that had started that morning worsened. I reclined and tried to doze. The contrast between Lynda's life in Phoenix and mine in Seattle hit me hard. If I were her, I'd be jealous or depressed. She didn't seem to be either. Her happiness for me oozed out of her in words and smiles. She beamed like a proud mother. When I tried to steer the conversation to her life she grumbled, but instead of being funny it fell flat.

Years later, I would look back on that four-day trip as the start of the period when everything changed. I'd remember well my confusion and unrest. The term "gut feel" isn't just a figure of speech.

7

NEW INFORMATION

AFTER I RETURNED to Seattle, I reversed my roles with Lynda and began to hunt down great cards, appropriate gifts, and music I thought she'd like. Her own impulsive buying had stopped, but her appreciation of my gifts increased. I set my buying ventures to once a month. She'd have something to look forward to if I baited her with, "Wait till you get the next package from me."

The suspense perked her up. She played the game. My new challenge became outdoing whatever I'd done the month before. It wasn't that easy. She no longer had sports in her life and her crankiness had increased.

Meanwhile, Todd remained in hiding in California, John worked more and more in his accounting practice, and Tim sloshed his way through bartending and partying.

"I'm disgusted with all of them," she said. "What's wrong with this generation, cookie? Or better question, what did I do wrong?"

I had no answers. I had no experience. Robin continued to amaze me with her competitive streak. She self-started, set goals, and worked hard. No one wanted to hear about all that goodness. No one would have believed I was an impartial observer. But I sat in awe much of the time and realized what a slug I'd been as a kid.

Lynda never bought that I had been that way. She saw some super-star who plowed straight through piles of shit looking madly for the pony, always believing there was one.

"You are the most positive person I have ever known," she said.

I smiled. "I don't know, Lynda. I'd say I'm more like the one who is just so stubborn I won't give up."

Either way—positive or negative—it was the person I let her see. The one I constructed and then tried to become.

Within a short time of moving to Seattle, I learned that the business climate was healthy and diverse, with thriving companies in aerospace, timber, medicine, and software. Enhancing that deeply capitalized base was an acceptance of women and minorities in all professions.

"Women are in power jobs everywhere," I told Lynda. "When I lived in Arizona, there was one woman in commercial real estate at one of the national firms. Here in Seattle at my firm, we have ten."

"Good for you, cookie. You girls should take over. The men have made a mess of everything," she said.

After winning "Rookie of the Year" at the end of my first year, I could see my progress and thrived with the recognition of my work. I continued to reset the bar, and I knew that my dream of becoming one of the top brokers in all of Seattle could happen one day.

"But you were the reason," Lynda said.

We debated. I did not want to disrespect the beginning of my business career in Arizona, but I remembered the good old boys network. It was the comparison of the two business climates that made it easy to come to the conclusion that Seattle was responsible for my success. I figured out that no matter what logic I presented to Lynda, she just wanted me to be her hero. It was an uncomfortable role for me.

Her interest and fascination with my job never lessened. She may have tired of hearing all the business points, but there was always interest in my clients' personalities. I focused excessively on the real estate side, the deal, and at first when she ventured questions about clients' age, background, physical characteristics, personality traits, education, or level of sophistication. I thought it was a waste of time. One time I told her about Henry, a man who had agreed to work with me on selling his five-acre piece which included a 75,000 square foot warehouse. Henry stiffened whenever we met, and I had no idea if he was uncomfortable with my recommendations or with me. He wouldn't open up. Lynda listened through my entire description of our conversations.

"What's his office like?" she asked. "What's on the wall? In his bookcases?"

I had to stop and think. There were no framed photos or other personal items that I could recall. "It's very neat but sterile. Except for the airplane stuff."

"Hmm. Have you ever asked him about it?" she said, then added, "Maybe he was a pilot, like your dad. Wouldn't that be something."

In the past, when I had tried to warm up our conversation, Henry had always changed the subject to the deal at hand, and since that seemed to be the subject with which he was most comfortable, I had followed his lead. Still, on my next visit I asked him about the prints.

He scooted his chair closer. "Those are planes I flew in the Air Force, World War II." He stared at the photos for a bit and shook his head. "That was a time."

"My dad was a Navy pilot in that war," I told him.

Henry quickly asked a myriad of questions, and our relationship changed that day. I felt it and he must have too. It would be the beginning of a mutually beneficial ten-year business alliance.

I began to think differently as each new deal started. Lynda loved her new role of counselor. When I told her I should be paying her referrals, she agreed.

A year went by before I saw her again. She had been unwilling to visit me, saying that the dampness didn't agree with her aching joints. When I told her about a trip to San Diego in the spring, she jumped on the offer to join us. We wanted Robin to enjoy better weather on her Easter break and to see some of California.

"Oh that fabulous zoo, restaurants in La Jolla, and the beaches. I can't wait, can't wait," she said. "And then there's seeing that little cookie II. What fun that will be."

At first Gary was less than enthusiastic about the arrangement. I explained that Lynda and Robin could share a room, thus giving us more privacy than we would have had otherwise. In a way, we had a built-in babysitter. He then thought it was a great idea. We would have six weeks to prepare for the trip. Meanwhile, Lynda called every other day with a new question.

Robin quizzed me as well. She loved the idea of Lynda joining our vacation. "Do you think Lynda might want to boogie board with me?" she wondered. Where she'd found out about boogie boarding I couldn't fathom, but it made me smile. "She didn't ask if I wanted to try it," I remarked to Gary.

He laughed. "She probably thinks you'd face plant into the beach," he said. "I might have to try it, though."

The day before we flew out, we confirmed our meeting places at the San Diego airport. I worried, even though Robin was already eleven and Lynda had traveled extensively. Lynda and I had not discussed her health in any detail and I considered how much difficulty she might have.

When I first spotted her, I didn't see the cane—not until she turned and limped toward me. I gasped. She shushed me and gave me a big hug and then one for Gary.

"Don't let it worry you. The damn thing is really making things more manageable for me even if it ruins my image," she said and laughed.

We still had thirty minutes before Robin's plane was scheduled to arrive. Gary moved to baggage claim while Lynda and I headed toward a bench to catch up. I wanted to know how long she had been using the cane. Did she feel worse? Had she been to the doctor? Should we get a wheelchair?

"So many questions. Geez. I'm okay. It's easier for me to get around with the cane. You know I don't like to be a burden to anyone," she said.

Her hair was shorter but longish in the back. It softened her look. She had a brighter smile, a relaxed expression.

New medication? Had the pain somehow diminished? I decided not to ask. I held her hand, completely delighted to see her. She shared a story about the young woman next to her on the flight from Phoenix—a porn star on tour.

"No way," I laughed. "The stories you invent."

"Swear to god, and get this? She's a tennis player at USC. The porn business is for extra cash, which she claimed is considerable. She's going to quit when she has a million," Lynda said.

"Well, all that experience with balls," I said. Lynda howled and reminded me what a bad girl I was.

Gary and a few others turned to see what was so funny. We quieted but continued our quips, snuffing out laughter. I thought it was too bad Gary was missing out on a conversation that would have fascinated him. On the other hand, it was a blessing Robin hadn't arrived yet.

I brought Lynda up to speed on news from Ohio. She remembered a lot about Robin's activities and told me that Robin had written to her the month before.

"What did she say?" I asked.

"She gave me advice on things I could do for my back. I really don't see how a Hula-Hoop could help, but she was adamant. It made me laugh. It's sweet that she's so concerned about an old lady."

Robin had never viewed Lynda as old. Mostly she referred to her as a "character." I'd grinned the first time she said it. It pleased me that she could be so right on at such a young age.

"I hope I recognize Robin," Lynda said and glanced at her watch. There was a crowd at gate 2. We learned that a soldier had transferred onto Robin's flight, coming home from overseas after almost two years. His family and friends had signs, balloons, flowers, and a trumpet player. They screamed and yelled, "Welcome home Larry!" Everyone cleared a path for the weary soldier as his eyes teared up.

Robin walked through the gang carrying what looked like a cat on her arm. It moved from side to side, looking at the people. Some laughed and a few squealed.

I hugged her and was about to ask how she'd gotten an animal on the plane when I realized it was a hand puppet. She worked it so well it sure looked real.

Lynda got a kick out of the thing and asked Robin its name.

"Rufus," Robin told her.

"Good choice. And did he behave on the plane?" Lynda said.

Robin scratched her head. Rufus looked up at Robin and then back at Lynda.

"Pretty much. He behaved about as well as I did."

The San Diego zoo was our first outing. I didn't need to worry about all the walking as Lynda rented a scooter and actually handled the whole day better than I did. Robin walked fast enough to keep up with her. They kept up a lively banter, often out of my earshot. Gary and I couldn't decide which of them was having more fun.

When we got to the monkeys and apes, Lynda opted to walk some. She pulled out her camera. "Robin, take a picture of me in front of my relatives."

Robin laughed so hard her hand shook and she had to take several shots. "That one to the left does look like you," she said. "But that one on the rock has your hair."

Later, at the Chart House restaurant, there was wine in chilled glasses, a bruschetta appetizer, a Shirley Temple for Robin even though she claimed she was too old for such a thing, and the Pacific Ocean crashing against the shoreline.

"What can we do tomorrow?" Robin asked, with a bit of let-down in her voice. It had been a hard day to surpass in enjoyment. All three of us eyed Gary.

"Sea World," Gary said. "Lynda might get picked to feed the whale. That would be interesting."

We laughed. Lynda dug in her purse and pulled out a prescription bottle. While we discussed Gary's idea she took two pills with a gulp of water.

I leaned toward her and said softly, "Is that something new?"

She nodded. "It works wonders. Percodan."

The name meant nothing to me. Still, she didn't have the drawn look on her face, no evidence of pinched nerve endings.

"How much do you take?" I gave her the once-over, as if I might find evidence of side effects.

She ignored me and turned to chat with Robin. They were never in short supply of things to discuss. Humorous observations followed by gales of laughter was the usual.

Gary touched my arm, "Something wrong?" I shrugged and let it go. Wrong time and place to talk about it.

Two days later we were sitting outside our La Jolla hotel enjoying a scrumptious breakfast. There was enough sunshine to keep us warm without our sweaters. Gary engulfed himself in the sports page while Lynda, Robin, and I attempted to solve the word jumble.

Suddenly Lynda announced, "I hate to leave this happy party but I've decided that I'll go home tomorrow. You three should have some time without the cripple."

Robin moved out of her chair and rested her arm around Lynda's shoulder. "No, you can't leave. We have more fun to do."

My mouth hung open. "Yes, why must you leave? Are you in pain? Did you get a phone call from Phoenix?"

Gary glanced up from his paper, confused. He hadn't heard a word but he sensed unhappy girls. He scooted his chair in closer and fixed his eyes on Lynda. She matched him like it was a contest.

"Lynda, I have a date for you tomorrow night," he said. She laughed in that knowing way—it wasn't true.

Our waitress appeared with more coffee. "Mas?" she asked Lynda and then Gary. When Maria was out of sight, Lynda tilted her head and nodded in the direction where she had walked.

"Do you think it would be good to be so young and beautiful? Having your whole life in front of you again?" Lynda said.

I didn't miss a beat. "No way. All that pain of figuring out who you really are and then dealing with it. I like where I am right now."

She sat back in her chair and squirmed, like she was trying to get more comfortable. "Instead of a date or even the idea of meeting a new man, I like the memory of the most perfect man I could have ever known, Peter. He was in my life long enough to bring me joy. Then, when he was gone, I still remembered that bliss. And who knows? Maybe someday I'll see him again."

Robin's face scrunched up as she followed the conversation. "You mean in heaven, right?"

Lynda knew that Robin and Sam attended church and studied the Bible ... I wondered how she'd answer.

"Only if I'm lucky," Lynda said. Gary and I laughed, and Robin's contorted face relaxed.

I drove Lynda to the airport for her early flight while Gary took Robin shopping for a new boom box. We giggled like a couple of teenagers about the four days of fun we'd shared.

"I liked the zoo the best," Lynda said. "It reminds me how much I prefer animals to humans."

California could test your patience with its traffic and sometimes strange people, but the view never disappointed anyone. Still, as much as I liked it, nothing about it seemed to resonate with what I would call home.

"How are you adjusting to Seattle?" Lynda asked me.

"Every day is better," I said. "I don't think I will ever get used to the idea of living there forever, but for now, it's fine," I said. "Maybe someday Gary will consider moving to Arizona."

We were within two miles of the airport. Lynda opened her mouth to speak, then stopped.

"What? Something wrong?" I said.

She sighed. "You'll be getting a subscription soon. I need to explain some things but we'll wait until you receive the first issue."

"Tell me now," I said.

She shook her head and sat up straighter in her seat. "I had the best time with you, Gary, and cookie II. It is fun to be around the three of you. You are so lucky and really—you deserve it Nancy. I can't tell you what a lift it was. Thank you so much for including me."

The departure drop-off neared. Sweat broke out on my forehead. We had either just avoided a serious conversation at the end of a visit or were at the start of something heavy. I felt the onset of an anxiety attack. I knew that she would not give me any more information, so I joined her in reminiscing and hugged her after I pulled up to the curb. She hesitated several seconds, as if she had another thought. Perhaps she considered saying something more.

"Call me when you get the issue." She got out of the car, then closed the door and blew me a kiss.

What in the hell was that all about?

Maybe Gary could make sense of it. Maybe he would interpret the whole thing in a way I hadn't thought of. I watched her hobble to the curbside check-in. I tried to be positive, but her remarks seemed ominous. Her words replayed in my mind and I tried to imagine what the subscription could possibly be. Occasionally I liked surprises, but not like this. And I would have to wait ... not in my gene pool.

Gary had no idea what Lynda had meant. He didn't seem concerned and even suggested that I had over-reacted. I wanted to believe him. I wanted to quit fretting and enjoy the rest of our vacation.

We had been back in Seattle for a week when a newspaper arrived in a brown wrapper. I tore it open. *The Hemlock Society* header stared back at me.

I fell into a kitchen chair. As clearly as I remembered Lynda's words, I hadn't considered anything like what appeared in front of me. I didn't know what to think, what to do, whom to call. Anger and sadness hit me in equal proportion.

What is she thinking? I started to pick up the paper and then pushed it away. Tears fell silently. Prince appeared and stared up at me. He circled and kept me in view. I picked him up and stroked his fur.

"We got trouble, Prince," I said. "She can't possibly mean this, can she? Off herself? Now what do I do?"

I called Gary's office but the receptionist said he had left for the day. I started to dial Lynda's number but hung up. There were no words to say to her. I sat and waited for wisdom, a sounding board, a decent idea. Anything.

"I have to call her but what in the hell am I going to say?" I said later to Gary. He listened to everything I could recall from our trip and my talks with Lynda. He didn't seem surprised or upset by the newspaper. Always calm and not quick to rush to a decision—a serious thinker, as Lynda had observed about him early on.

"Maybe she's exploring options," he said. "You know, if things continue to worsen. And even then, exactly what is meant by sending this newspaper is unknown to us. She did say that the Percodan worked well, a miracle drug for her. Let's not get too upset."

For a while I felt better. Maybe I had rushed to interpret the meaning of Lynda's gesture; maybe she was simply considering future options. I tossed the newspaper aside and busied myself with wifely duties: making dinner, doing a load of laundry, feeding Prince, and rearranging my spices, which somehow had gotten out of alphabetical order. Mundane chores always helped me regain balance. By bedtime I felt more in charge and less stressed. Gary's logic made sense.

Bad dreams and restless sleep interrupted the calm. At work, I could not focus, and there was plenty of drama to keep me nervous as it was. Right in the middle of my first multi-million deal, the buyer had gone non communiqué. No phone calls or faxes returned; not seen at his office in two days. Full on panic kept me maniacal. I wanted to call Lynda in the worst way, to hear her joke about my superstition that everything—good and bad—happened in threes. But I couldn't call her because she'd bring up the newspaper, and then what would I say about that? Besides, I thought, it was selfish to call her with my problem when hers was potentially life-threatening, or life-deciding.

The next few days stayed fogged over and then, sunshine. My buyer showed up with a valid explanation. A few hours later, Lynda called me at work.

"Cookie, I haven't heard from you. Did you receive the newspaper yet?" Lynda said as if she were asking what the weather was like.

The sound of her voice made my stomach pitch and roll.

I covered the mouthpiece with my hand and lowered myself into my chair. "And what is this supposed to mean? That you're contemplating drastic measures?"

My voice cracked and the words came out louder than I wanted.

"Oh for heaven's sake," Lynda said. "I know I can be a drama queen, but I have just been reading up on their views. The Hemlock Society is out there, no? I really just wanted your opinion on the articles, especially the one called 'Whose Life Is It, Anyway?'"

"This whole thing creeps me out, if you want to know the truth," I said. "People don't talk about death."

The phone line scratched. I waited a second to see if she was still there. There was a light cough. "The article that I mentioned is on the front page. Maybe you could read it and then call me."

Her tone, which had started out light and breezy, had morphed into that of a serious journalist. The hairs on my arms stood up, like they were full of electricity. All the relief I had felt earlier when my buyer called had vanished. I wanted to scream or throw up. I held the phone against my ear unable to say a word. Two guys walked by my cubicle laughing and jostling each other.

"Hello?" Lynda said.

I let out the biggest sigh without covering the mouthpiece. Maybe I did it to let her know my frustration or maybe I couldn't think clearly. Telephone etiquette wasn't on my mind. I wanted to solve her problem and so far, I had failed. Every suggestion had been a dead end, every month left Lynda in more pain, every doctor had thrown in the towel. I slouched back in my chair and rocked. I stared out into space.

"Of course I'll read it," I said softly. I pictured her smiling because her voice softened when she said okay. After we hung up I sat. And sat.

That night I read the article quickly. Then I went out for a four-mile run, something to ease the anxiety. Nothing about Derek Humphry's stance was controversial; rather I agreed with the Hemlock Society's founder. His underlying principle was that each person owns his life, and each should be able to decide when it's time to leave. He cited how humane we are when it comes to our animals but that we have different rules for people. Nevertheless, his justification of suicide left me unsettled.

Reason and emotion fought for control over my mind. I ran faster but nothing calmed me. If I agreed with the writer, then the natural conclusion of suicide—what he called self-deliverance—had merit. I tried to put myself in Lynda's place. If I were her, would my desire to live trump the pain I had to endure? Would I feel I had enough in my life to make the struggle worth it? It was impossible to know. I had never had the kind of pain she had lived with for years. Whenever I got sick, a doctor fixed it. The most precious thing I had in my life was love—for

Robin, Gary, and the rest of my family. Love might not be the only things that made my world go round, but it had made the ride interesting.

Lynda's words about what made a meaningful life came back to me: "someone to love, work you enjoy, and something to look forward to." I certainly had that. She'd had it when Peter was alive. Afterwards, she had bits and pieces. And now, the pain overtook all.

"What would you do?" I asked Gary.

He sat with Prince in his lap and petted him. I summarized the article, but there was anger and emotion in my version. He didn't answer right away, as was his nature.

"I have no idea," he finally said. "There is no way to put myself in Lynda's place. However, I do believe in quality of life over quantity. To stay alive just to be here—that would never be what I'd want."

Prince was our diversion during this time. When we came to an impasse or a flat-out disagreement, we could always come back together over our attention and love for him. He seemed to sense his role as diplomat. He'd stare at whoever held him and then look to the other, careful to give equal time. Sometimes we'd talk through him to each other. Gary would say something like, "Prince, tell your mother I'm sorry," and then the cat would gaze up at me. It worked every time.

On the last of the three reads through the article, I made notes in the margins and reread a highlighted part: "Everyone wants a calm death. Very few have it. The only guarantee is to plan it yourself."

I knew Lynda awaited my call, anxious, and yet I procrastinated. Gary noticed the newspaper had all of my attention but said nothing until the next evening. Perhaps he thought I was just an incredibly slow reader: it was not like me to avoid confrontation.

"When do you plan to talk to her?" he said. It irritated me. I snapped at him; he shrugged and left the room. I followed him and apologized.

What is wrong with me?

"Don't worry about it," he said and gave me an undeserved hug. "You have a lot on your mind right now. I get it."

Sleep didn't come quickly that evening and when it did, I tossed about for the rest of the night. By the time I raised my sorry ass out of bed, Gary was long gone. As I brushed my teeth, a dream from the night before came back to me. It was actually a rehash of a childhood trauma.

Our first dog, Nelly, was a lovable great pyrenees. I was only four years old when Dad brought her home as a puppy. She had a sweet disposition and followed us everywhere. Five years later, she was struck by a car and lay in pain while we waited for the vet. She moaned, her eyes roling back in her head. I was nine years old and my brother, Richie, was seven. We huddled around her and cried.

The vet was a kind and gentle man. When he moved his thick fingers slowly around Nelly's body, her moans increased. She had not moved from the position where Dad had laid her out in the barn. I saw the vet shaking his head at Dad.

"We shouldn't let her suffer, Rich."

Dad eyes watered. He nodded.

The vet dug into his bag. Dad took Richie and me by the hand. He sat down outside and put each of us on a knee. My tears hadn't stopped, nor had Richie's.

"Nelly is in a lot of pain. She is not going to get well. The vet is going to put her to sleep so that she won't hurt anymore. I want you both to say good-bye to her. She has been a great dog to us."

Dad wiped our tears. He took us back in the barn where we all knelt down beside Nelly. She looked peaceful. The vet kept a hand on her head. Quickly her eyes shut and her body went limp.

We buried Nelly on the farm right beside a huge lilac bush. Dad told us to visit her grave and talk to her any time we wanted. Richie and I wondered if Dad ever did such a thing because we never saw him go out there. The two of us often knelt at the mound, and it became a refuge in times of trouble in later years.

Humaneness. That's what I learned on the farm. Nelly wasn't the only casualty during those years. I remembered it all clearly. Slowly I moved toward the phone and dialed. Lynda answered on the second ring.

"Nancy doll, I am so glad to hear your voice."

You do not know how far you can be stretched until someone pulls your internal rubber band, until circumstances test your beliefs, until no matter how logical your reasoning may be there is no solution, until you try with all your might to walk in someone else's shoes and experience the pain of every step. That's what happened to me. I had to lose sleep; I had to read everything I could, which often led to more discomfort; I had to pray to whomever for guidance, for the courage to be a good friend. I needed strength. Inside I wavered but outwardly I listened; I tried to be the same person I had always been. That was what Lynda deserved.

I wished I had someone to consult, someone who wouldn't moralize. I wanted a woman to share my anguish, but there was none. Instead, the topic of "self-deliverance" became the meat of every conversation with Lynda. Not easy. Humor, if there was any, came from a dark place. Each conversation left me depleted, lower than the one before. Her tunnel vision became emotional baggage for me, but I started to hear in a new way. She no longer wanted my opinions and there was nothing left to discuss. I let her do the talking.

When *Top Gun* came out, I insisted that she go see it. Lynda had always loved movies, but lighthearted pursuits seemed to have been put on permanent hold. I wanted to restore them. She humored me. "Okay, okay I'll hobble to Harkins Theatre tomorrow. Do I have to report back? Write the review?"

"This is Tom Cruise's breakout movie," I said. "Instead of the kid in *Risky Business*, he's now a sex symbol, or so the reviews say. I know how much you like handsome guys."

She called the next day, right after she saw it. The plot, the music, the airplane action, the love story—all of it filled her up. She claimed she forgot about every ache and pain. "I think Cruise may have a future," she predicted. We laughed.

Encouraged by her upbeat tone, I told her I had other suggestions for entertainment, but she scoffed.

"Important decisions have all my attention right now," she said. "A well-thought-out plan will give me the peace I need. After that, the only thing left will be the courage to execute it."

Shivers coursed through my whole body. My tear ducts were empty. We were at the end of the rope and all I could do was hold on while Lynda swung.

Within a week or so, another package arrived from the Hemlock Society. A book, *Let Me Die Before I Wake*, by Derek Humphry. I threw it on the floor and paced. Prince trailed me from room to room. I gathered him up and moved to the deck. Some distance below, cars whizzed by. Beyond that, the natural beauty of Lake Sammamish, one mile wide and eleven miles long. Water skiing enthusiasts clamored for a spot during the summertime. My mind drifted as a sleek cigarette-style boat powered by. Normally I would have rated the paint job or how fast the boat glided across the water, but today I hardly noticed. Prince leaped up on the railing of the deck, ever vigilant and on the lookout for birds, squirrels, a mouse, or another cat. While he played master hunter, I pouted.

Two days passed before I read the book in one sitting. Chapter One began: "Why are so many people more readily appalled by an unnatural form of dying than by an unnatural form of living?"

Wow was all I could think as I finished the last page.

"What if a greater power thinks it's wrong?" I said to Lynda. "I mean, what if this is some kind of test, merely to get to the next dimension?"

She coughed in an exasperated way. Then she said, "I'll tell you what. I won't do anything until you're okay with it."

Let Me Die Before I Wake was a skinny book, but the subject matter was heavy and final. It depressed me but seemed to give Lynda confirmation. She became a devoted advocate with a plan.

"Are you with me?" she finally asked.

No brainy idea surfaced. Each conversation pushed me further toward acceptance, but she wanted me to get it and was willing to wait for me. The pressure mounted as I felt enormous disgust with the topic.

"What exactly is it that you want from me? I can't stand all this discussion much more," I said. "It doesn't seem natural to have a calm discussion about suicide. It just isn't."

"Self-deliverance," she corrected me softly.

I wanted to hang up. Then I felt like a shitty friend. It was her life, hers that was so rotten she wanted to end it. I knew about the pain that had lasted years, the dead-end searches for a cure to give her some kind of acceptable existence. I knew how alone she was, how cut off from her sons, how nothing about each day held a minute of promise. There was no joy left in her life.

"Do you think I'm a coward?" Her voice barely audible.

"No. In fact, I think suicide—sorry, self-deliverance—takes enormous courage. I can't imagine doing it myself."

Silence filled the phone line. I heard her breathe. She mumbled something to George before her attention returned.

"I'd like to take one last trip. Just you and me for a few days. Could you come to Phoenix?"

My stomach churned. "There's a lot going on right now, but I could come in October some time."

"That's too late," she said. "I plan to be gone by early August."

8

FINAL GOOD-BYE

THE FLIGHT TO Phoenix gave me time to ready myself as much as I could for what I thought would be impossible: to enjoy one last adventure with my best friend without thinking about what was going to happen. I rubbed my temple remembering all of our debates, which only seemed to deepen her conviction. Those conversations had been the norm for months and months until the worst of all, our most recent talk, which had become a heated exchange unlike any I'd ever been a party to. She made some cavalier comment about her "self-deliverance" that exploded inside me.

"I have had it with all this talk about how great death will be. Is there no reason for you to stay on the planet? Not even one? Why kill yourself at fifty-six? Somehow it seems like the easy way out, not how I think of you. Where is your pride?" I screamed. I'm sure my tone stunned her, as she remained silent. I took a breath and continued, "And just how sick are you, really?"

Mild static filled the phone lines. I hadn't planned to say any of those words or play the pride card. As a businesswoman who usually stayed in control, adversity and unreasonable people were my forte, and yet I had failed. The situation wasn't fixed, she remained broken, and I would be left without her. Maybe I hoped to jolt her enough that she'd see a spark in her life. Perhaps if I made her angry enough, she would fight. In desperation, I used my silver bullet.

She didn't hang up. She said nothing. I waited.

"Nancy, I have done everything I can think of to explain myself to you. It's enough already," she finally said. Her voice remained calm, relieved. "The pain is more than I've told you, way more. And nothing has changed in a year, except that I'm more determined than ever. I want to quit while I'm behind."

Neither of us spoke. She probably recalled my comment about how the first person to speak loses. I waited but so did she.

She exhaled long. "Good health notwithstanding, everyone needs three things: someone to love, work they enjoy, and something to look forward to. Sound familiar?"

I twisted the phone cord around my index finger, nodding at her famous quote. Who could argue with that?

We'd ended the conversation with tears and promises. I pictured her smiling as she said, "I don't want to have another debate. All of that is over. I only want to make a plan for a final vacation with my friend. My treat. After all, you did give me an extra year, with all of your humor and obnoxious arguing." She laughed. "But now I'm ready. And there is only one rule for this vacation: no talk about death. And most important: no crying. Got it?"

"No problem," I said. "I understand."

Baggage claim at Sky Harbor was jammed. In August, yet. Everyone jockeyed for position as luggage rolled around on the carousel. As soon as I grabbed my bag, I headed outdoors where we agreed to meet. Her sparkling clean Firebird sat right in front.

Settled in the car she looked almost the same as the first time we met. I hugged her and caught a whiff of Johnson's baby powder, her favorite. For a second I thought I would cry. She must have felt it.

"It's okay," she whispered in my ear. "This weekend will be like old times. I even have some surprises."

We sat for a few seconds and looked into each other's eyes. It didn't feel sad or sentimental.

She pulled out into traffic. I glanced outside at the scruffy desert vegetation that dotted both sides of the freeway. The driest time of the year. Everything looked in need of water, impossible to get in summer.

"The car hasn't aged a bit," I said hoping to find some humorous topic to divert attention.

"Still wash it every other day and wax it once a quarter. That'll be a savings," she said. "You don't by any chance want it, do you? 'Cause I'd love for you to have it."

I shook my head. She reached over for my hand and squeezed it for a second. Thoughts bounced around my brain like the balls in a lottery machine. I twirled a lock of hair around my finger. I tapped my fingers on the center console. Suddenly Lynda veered off to the side of the road, cutting in front of a semi. Cars honked and whizzed by.

"What the hell?" I said.

She glared at me. "I need you to be strong. We already covered this. I am counting on you."

I dropped my head but just for a moment. She was right. Somewhere I offered up a little prayer to anyone who could hear. I wanted stamina and resolve.

She waited for traffic to clear. "We're stopping at the house just for a few minutes and then we are going on to Rio Rico. There are some things to tidy up before our trip."

There had been much more development around Ahwatukee since the year before. What had been the last stop in the middle of nowhere now boasted shops, office buildings, and a school.

She hit the garage door opener on her visor as she drove south on Shoshoni Drive. Her place was still five houses away.

"I think you actually have to be in front of the garage," I said.

"Hey cookie, you're supposed to be respectful of me in my pre-gone condition," she said. Then she added, "Actually, I've always been curious how close you have to be to make it open."

I laughed. "Just now you're wondering?"

She poked me. "You take stock of many things near the end. Sometimes serious, sometimes goofy."

The empty garage spooked me. Only a water softener occupied a small corner of the space that used to house a masterful collection of Christmas decorations, luggage, garden tools, extra light bulbs, toilet paper, wrapping paper and gift boxes, golf clubs, tax records labeled by year, pet cages, flattened moving boxes, seasonal table decorations, and other assorted paraphernalia.

"It didn't seem fair to make the boys go through all my junk," Lynda said. "They're off on their own lives now. I gave things away like crazy and tossed the rest."

The details of her grand plan had been spoken in part. I never made it through all she wanted to say. I squirmed in my seat, afraid to make eye contact. She touched my sweaty hand.

"My famous margarita awaits. C'mon." She slid out of her seat.

Fresh squeezed lime juice, Lynda's secret ingredient, soothed me. It smelled as good as it tasted. I sipped and tried to get comfortable in uncharted territory. A decent night's sleep had eluded me for five days, and the dark circles under my eyes proved it. Gary had only taken me to SeaTac airport that morning after much protest. He thought I worked too hard and had succumbed to Lynda's demand for a visit at the most inopportune times. Somehow I assured him that there was no reason to be concerned. Lynda had asked for secrecy about the finality of our last trip, and I gave it to her. She wanted to ensure that no one would interfere with her decision. That element added to my stress. I felt like an actress who finally believes her own bullshit.

Lynda disappeared into her bedroom. I glanced around the kitchen and family room that we had worked on so diligently. The plush tan sectional and pale yellow walls were inviting. She had said she wanted cheery. Her art had been collected over a twenty-year period and reflected her eclectic taste: the modern oversized oil of a barely recognizable horse that I'd seen on my first visit to her villa, a numbered Degas print, and a Renoir-like watercolor. A massive wall unit held hundreds of her favorite books. *To Kill a Mockingbird, Gone With the Wind, Atlas Shrugged,* and Shakespeare's *Complete Works* claimed their places of honor on the top shelf. Other collectables were a bronze cowboy statue, two Navajo baskets, and artifacts from travels to New Zealand, London and Italy. A Sony television and her stereo system were the only ordinary elements. She had the same diverse taste in music: Mozart, Andy Williams, Linda Ronstadt, the Boston Pops, Fleetwood Mac and lots of old rock 'n' roll.

I smiled, remembering all the laughs we'd had picking out the paint color, shopping for perfect lamps, and arranging the real plants.

Lynda dropped a Sakowitz shopping bag in front of me. "Let's go to the table."

At first I thought it was a gift. She had spoiled me over the years with so many unexpected and generous presents—a graphite tennis racket, a St. John's knit dress from Neiman Marcus, a matching 14K gold necklace and earrings—all because she thought they suited me. She delighted in the surprise of a no-occasion gift.

But this time, a somber look on her face instantly warned of something else. She motioned for me to open it.

I removed a pair of white cotton gloves and then a wooden box. It puzzled me and I shrugged. She kept eye contact. When I stopped and sat back in my chair she urged me on. My hands shook as I lifted the lid.

A gleaming silver gun stared back at me. I slammed the box shut and pushed it toward Lynda. She remained still.

"I don't think I can get the Seconal I need," she said. "If my contact doesn't come through soon, then it's the surest and quickest solution. A .38 caliber," she said. I picked up my drink.

The air-conditioner clicked on. A rush of cool air hit my body. I had no words. No thoughts. No comment.

"I know this will sound odd, but if I can think of the gun as my friend, then I won't feel so anxious," she said. "Right now it's a powerful monster. But I don't want to think of it that way."

I scowled. It was the most ridiculous thing I'd ever, ever heard. She ignored me and kept on talking.

"You could help me name him. A common name that's as comfortable as slippers you've worn for ten years," she said.

The start of a full-blown headache pounded behind my eyeballs. I reached for my purse. Three Tylenol at least, and that was only if I'd caught it soon enough. I washed them down with some of the margarita.

"How about Frank?" I said. "Your friend Frank. The alliteration probably appeals to you."

She smiled then and petted the box like a dog. "Are you still afraid of guns?"

My refusal to answer hinted at my revulsion.

"Please. It would really help me if you'd put the gloves on and hold it. Just hold it. Please," her voice cracked.

In slow motion I eased my right hand into one of the gloves. Then my left. I held them up for her inspect. It was a stall tactic. I cleared my throat, took a deep breath, and reached for the gun.

The lightness of it startled me. I moved it back and forth between my hands. I flipped it over. The sides were a brushed metal with pearl inlays. I studied the trigger. Finally, I rotated the gun back toward me and peered down the barrel. I had never seen a gun up close.

I gulped the air. A heavy metal smell overwhelmed me. Thoughts of smoke and blood sparked through my brain. I quickly returned the gun to the box and removed the gloves. The whole thing made me queasy. I couldn't look at her, my best friend. She handed me my margarita and I chugged it.

Miracle of miracles, I didn't cry. I didn't say a word. I kept my emotions in check and sat. What else was coming? It was almost comical, this new information overload.

Lynda put the Sakowitz bag away. She then took me to her oversized walk-in closet and encouraged me to pick out tennis outfits. Even though we wore different sizes, she insisted I make some selections. The closet was nearly empty, aside from twenty or so tennis skirts and a few other items. The long dresses, shoes, sandals, jackets, sweaters, purses, straw hats, and visors—all gone. To humor her, I selected two of her favorite skirts, which she liked. She even offered that my tennis game might improve, via transference.

I plopped down on her bed and sighed. She joined me and handed over a manila envelope.

"One last thing. I've been saving this for you," she said.

Now what? I'm about to implode.

I opened it and saw stacks and stacks of hundred-dollar bills. My mouth fell open. "What the hell?"

"I didn't want Timothy to give your ring to another girl. You know, some day that could happen. Anyhow, I bought it from him and then put it in a jewelry store on consignment. They found a buyer. Since the ring was for you, so is the money," she said.

I shook my head. Finally, it really was too much. I handed it back to her.

"Think of it as your inheritance then, if that makes it easier for you," she said. "End of discussion. C'mon, let's get a move on."

Once we were on the road headed to Rio Rico, things got better. Lynda insisted I drive. It was my last and final duty. I suddenly thought about Nora and asked Lynda if we'd be seeing her.

"Of course. She'll be with us tonight for dinner, and then it's just you and me," Lynda said.

We merged onto I-10, and after she made herself as comfortable as possible, she began to reflect. She wanted to hear my most treasured memory of her.

It was an easy question and I think she knew I'd pick Carlos at the Westward Look. I still giggled just thinking about it. Definitely her finest hour.

"Tell me again what the people in the audience said. You know," she said. "The good stuff."

We relived the serenade, the tennis tournament against Goldilocks and her partner, and the rest of that trip. We could have gone on rehashing those events for as long as it had taken us to live them.

Rio Rico hadn't changed much in four years. The only difference was there were even fewer people than there had been the first time I went there. The place was still well maintained, but it was losing its charm somehow. I said nothing about that and instead effused over the landscaping, the attention from the staff, and the fresh flowers all over the lobby.

We were given what was called a junior suite, with a separate area for the television and a wet bar as well as an outside deck with comfortable lounge chairs. The eastern exposure shielded us from the late afternoon sun, allowing us to enjoy the view surrounding the gardens and pool. Lynda pulled a bottle of wine from the bar and had me pour us each a glass over ice because she always wanted it colder than just chilled. She grabbed a bag of salted cashews, even though in the past she'd always groused about the exorbitant markup in hotels on such items.

"To you, cookie," she said and raised her glass. "All of my very best to you, Gary, and cookie II. May you be happy and healthy forever."

"To girlfriends. Best of friends," I said and tipped my glass toward her.

She smiled and sipped. Finally we both agreed that despite the great view, it wasn't worth sitting in 110-degree heat. We headed inside and flipped on the TV. She always wanted to see a recap of the daily news.

"How about one of my famous foot massages while we watch the news?" I said. She immediately ditched her shoes and propped her feet up on the couch.

I grabbed some lotion and set to work on her gnarled feet. She oohed and aahed as I rubbed and kneaded the balls of her feet, then the arches. Every once in a while she added her two cents to the news anchor's narration.

"Too bad you were never in television," I said. "You might have been controversial, but what drama you would have added."

She nodded. Then a sigh.

We rested and finished our wine. Lynda wanted an early dinner. I teased her that she was too young to go to the dining room at six, much less five. She liked that and said that she thought she could make it until six thirty.

"Nora likes to eat early all the time," she said. "She'd meet me at six."

"Bet you already told her to meet us at six, didn't you?"

There were so many view tables it took us a while to pick one. Nora picked one in the farthest corner, then Lynda changed us twice before she was satisfied. We ordered wine and a bruschetta appetizer—I sensed both of them were starving.

"I think we should have our own smorgasbord," Lynda proposed. "You each pick a couple of things and so will I. We don't have to eat it all."

Right after our delicious salads—the first course of many—she ordered champagne. I protested but to no avail. I hoped all the food would soak up the extra alcohol—I'd had more than I was used to.

Once the waiter filled our flutes, Nora raised her glass, "To Lynda, my very special friend. I'll always love you."

Lynda kept eye contact with Nora and nodded. It was a private moment; everything felt serious all of the sudden.

"Hey what about me?" I said.

Lynda broke the stare. "Oh yes, you too, cookie."

The waiter helped our celebration with impeccable service and a charming personality. "Ladies, I want you to have the best time tonight," he said.

"We will," Lynda said and smiled.

Maybe the waiter was calculating his potential tip. I should have told him to address Lynda by name as many times as possible, and he'd be guaranteed twenty percent.

There was so much food left on the table at the end that it looked as if we hadn't taken a bite. A few people stared at us. Lynda said to ignore them. It took some time to clear the table, after much discussion about what to do with the leftovers. Nora said she knew a family who would love to have the doggie bags.

"Are you sure it's not for Leon and tomorrow night's dinner?" Lynda said. "Not that I mind."

Nora laughed and shook her head. "No way. He eats cereal."

"Ladies, what else can I get you? Coffee? An after dinner drink?" the waiter said patiently.

"Dessert menus, please." Lynda gave him her slyest grin.

I shook my head. There wasn't an ounce of room left in my stomach. I wanted to take off my too-tight jeans right there.

Lynda ordered a chocolate mousse cake, an apple pie with cinnamon ice cream, and a strawberry parfait. The dumbfounded expression on the waiter's face was priceless.

"What?" Lynda said. Nora and I couldn't quit laughing.

When we got to the lobby, Nora stopped and turned to Lynda. She took Lynda's hand and put it over her heart. "I shall keep you with me always." Lynda nodded. Nora continued, "Do not be afraid."

I felt like an intruder in their most private moment. Nora finally turned to me. "Waddle her back to the room, will you, Nancy?"

Lynda and I watched her leave and then headed back to the elevator. Neither of us spoke until we got to our room.

"Why didn't you stop me, cookie?" Lynda groaned as she rubbed her tummy. I flipped on the TV and we fell onto our beds. We quickly bored with the news and tuned in to a movie in progress. *Back to the Future* was just the medicine we needed. We laughed and then sighed. Within thirty minutes, Lynda fell asleep in her clothes. When the movie ended I got up and went through my nightly ritual. She snored and looked so comfortable that I took her shoes off and let her be.

Sleep came fast and hard. I didn't wake up during the night and I didn't have nightmares. I woke up refreshed and full of energy. It was after nine o'clock. Lynda was on her side in pajamas. That surprised me because I hadn't heard a sound during the night. I gently removed the covers and tiptoed to the closet for my running gear. I was dressed, shoes on, teeth brushed, contact lenses in place and almost out the door when she whispered, "Hey you, I'm starving. Don't be gone too long." Then she giggled.

Breakfast was more reasonable. Just toast, coffee, and a small orange juice. I applauded her restraint.

"I should probably give you some pointers on gin rummy," she said out of nowhere. "Card games always come in handy. And frankly, you are a terrible gin player."

"Ouch," I said as I slapped my hand over my heart. "I beat you a few times. C'mon, remember?"

She leaned toward me. "Big secret. I let you win."

We spent the rest of the morning and early afternoon poolside while she instructed and then tested me on her system. The basics were a visualization technique of the four suits and checking off cards as they appeared. It was true that she'd always been a heck of a good card player. She'd told me once that she and Peter had been great bridge partners. Her method wasn't that hard, really. But the brain drain and sun made me sleepy.

That evening we were welcomed by the same waiter, who chuckled as he approached our table. "Ladies, welcome back. The chef has an assistant tonight. We are ready for you."

Lynda loved his teasing. She assured him that we weren't going to repeat our spectacle of the night before. We skipped appetizers and wine, and settled for fish, a salad, and iced tea.

"What was your proudest moment?" I asked after the waiter left. "And I don't mean of Peter or one of the kids. Something that was yours."

She played with a spoon and looked off into the distance. "The first time Bell and I won. He was the one who knew we could win, I'm convinced. His strength and class gave me so much. There's just nothing like the first time, when the odds were against us."

Her eyes watered for a moment. She dabbed them with a napkin. I wanted to honor all she cherished from her life. Talk about it, remember it, have her remind me about the important events she'd already shared with me. It was her time.

She reflected on many things. I listened. We stayed in the restaurant three hours, which had never happened before. Maybe we were trying to stop the clock, extend the little remaining time we had, forget for a moment the end was coming.

On the last morning, we slept late again. Lynda decided she wanted to drive north to Tubac and spend the day there. The artist colony held special memories for her from her from her travel days with Peter. I thought that the place had become more of a tourist trap than an artist haven and was afraid it would depress her, but I supported her wish. The only problem would be the walking. Once we arrived there, we ambled around, but my fears proved correct—the town bored us.

"Where was your favorite artist's studio?" I asked.

She perked up a little and pointed down a nearby alley. I suggested we take a look, not thinking it would still be there, just to get her into a good place, so she could reflect on something pleasant and fun. She used the cane on her right side and let me hold her left arm as we made our way. She began a story about Wally, the guy who used to own the studio.

All of the sudden she stopped and gasped.

"Oh my god. He's still there!" She pointed with her cane. If an artist studio gets points for being disheveled, in serious disrepair, Wally scored an A. Lynda's pace increased. The door was open.

"Wally?" she said as we entered.

There was no response. A fan whirred overhead, but it didn't help. It was hot and sticky. Bronze statues of all sizes stood in disarray, some on the floor, a few on the counter, more on rickety shelves. Lynda called out again.

"Be right there," a male voice yelled. "I'm indisposed."

Lynda and I laughed. In no time, a heavily bearded hippie guy appeared. His thin body and pale skin didn't fit what I had pictured. He had the lightest blue eyes I'd ever seen, nearly translucent.

"Lynda-lou, sweet Jesus. How the hell are you?" he tried to hug her around the cane. She made quick introductions.

"Any friend of Lynda is a friend of mine," he said. "What's this?" he turned back to look at the cane.

"Just some back trouble," she said. "It's nothing."

They caught each other up to date. I ambled around the studio and tried to be invisible. The pieces were remarkable, but Wally was in serious need of order. Marketing. I figured he didn't care about that.

Lynda called out from across the room to ask if I'd get her a cold drink down the street. I disappeared on my errand. It seemed like a good idea to give them privacy, so I took my time returning.

"What do you think, Nancy?" Lynda asked when I came back with her Coke. Wally was polishing up a bronze cowboy statue that stood on the counter.

"I like it," I said. "It looks a lot like the one you already have, though."

"It's for you," she said. Wally smiled and took money from Lynda. I gasped. I'd glimpsed the price tag, and it said $750.

We ended up having a light lunch with Wally. He had no problem closing the studio for an hour. There wasn't much traffic in August and besides, he said, he hadn't had a decent meal in several days.

"How much longer can the bronze Western stuff be popular?" he said as his eyes twinkled. "All the California people who keep moving here don't want this."

"Oh Wally, you'll always be a hit," Lynda said.

"I'm serious," Wally said and leaned toward Lynda. "Last week a lady came in here and poked around for a bit. She wanted to know where I tied up my horse."

All of us laughed. I wondered if it was true, but once again I was taken in by a master storyteller. The hour went by in a split second. There were so many questions I wanted to ask him, but he and Lynda had a good old time talking about people and things of which I knew nothing. I let it go. It was great to see her smile and enjoy herself.

For our last dinner at Rio Rico, we were greeted by the same waiter, and that was too funny. We all laughed. "Conversation or food tonight?" he asked.

We took the same table as we had the previous nights, and since I couldn't imagine what to order, I decided to let Lynda pick for both of us. She loved the idea. It inspired her to ask for special preparations, and the waiter seemed happy to oblige.

"What if I don't like it?" I worried, feeling the beginning of a pout. "I am a bit of a picky eater."

She grimaced. "Tell me something I don't know, Dick Tracy."

In return, I got to pick the desserts—three of them, again. Chocolate in everything, that was my criteria.

The next morning, on the way back to Phoenix, we talked about my mother and all the progress she and I had made in our relationship. Lynda complimented me on tolerance but then she warned me, "If you forgive your enemies but still remember their names, I don't know cookie ... I think you still have work to do."

Once again, she got right to the heart of the matter. She often had the unpleasant task of force-feeding me. I had to stop and think. Stop and reconsider. Stop and hopefully change.

"Who will be my teacher?" I said. My throat dried up.

"Simple. I'll talk to you in your dreams. Not to worry. And if you want to talk to me, then pose your question just before you go to sleep."

I almost drove the Firebird off the road. Where in the heck had that come from? It didn't sound like her. Spiritual stuff had always been a topic of ridicule.

But I knew she was serious. It actually made me feel better.

When you think a drive will take forever and you want it to, then that for sure will be the quickest trip of your life. In no time we were within Phoenix city limits and heading for the airport. We quieted. Lynda turned off the radio. I saw her out of the corner of my eye. She looked straight ahead.

I took the airport exit and veered off to passenger unloading. Words were failing me. Sweat trickled from my chin and ran down my neck. I wiped my whole face with my sleeve.

"What a great journey we've had," she said and clasped my hand. We both continued to stare ahead while the car idled.

"Thank you, dear Lynda, for all of your support, love, and help to me and Robin. Gary too," I said. I saw her nod but we still didn't look at each other.

"Can I go now?" she whispered.

I turned to look at her. It wasn't my right, to give my permission. How could she ask me this?

"It's the last thing I'll ask you for, I promise."

"Okay," I said and turned away. There was nothing else to add.

She cleared her throat. Without a glance in my direction she said, "Some day when you tell my story, and I know you will, just remember—I want to be tall."

EPILOGUE

LYNDA'S LAST ENTRY in her diary read, "This is it, I hope. I love all my beautiful young people and thank God—they love me. 8/6/86. I wish I understood numerology."

She died, on August 6, 1986, by her own hand. Golfers found her in the backyard, away from the house. Tim called me to deliver the news. "She's gone, Nancy." His shaky voice broke me but I couldn't cry, even though I wished I could.

"What are the plans?" I finally asked.

"She'll be cremated, she already arranged it. Just John, Nora, and me at the cemetery," he said barely aloud. "And you too, if you want."

I stared out the window of my house and pulled on the telephone cord. Somewhere a clock ticked.

"I won't be coming," I told him. "I already said my good-bye."

When the tears came an hour later, I thought they would never stop. I screamed, cursed, and stomped around the empty house. Prince raced ahead of me for safety.

My body ached, my head throbbed, and my stomach upended. Never had I felt so alone, not even when Dad had died. I finally climbed the stairs, collapsed into bed, and sank into a depression that lasted for days. I didn't go to work, I didn't call in, I didn't eat. Gary tried everything. "Please, just leave me alone," I said so many times that eventually he did.

When I stopped to get a good look at myself, I gasped. "This is not what Lynda would want at all," I muttered to myself. "What a mess you are!"

A week passed before I remembered Lynda's instruction. One night, when I was just about to go to bed and Gary was out of earshot, I asked her a simple question, "Are you okay, Lynda?"

That night she smiled at me in a dream. She looked radiant, younger than the first time I'd met her. "I'm good, cookie. It was the right thing."

I slept through the whole night and awoke refreshed, without stress or sadness.

Nora and I talked about a month later. I wanted to discuss everything that had happened but I could tell she didn't. It was too hard. "The bravest woman I have ever known," Nora said. "She'll be missed but never forgotten. Never."

I still talk to Lynda. She hasn't lost one iota of spunk. She likes to lecture, remind me of funny things that I did in the past, and kicks my ass when I'm whining or dragging my feet to get something done. Every year on her birthday, October 16, I visit her at the cemetery and we have an extra long talk. For the first several years it was sad, but not now. She doesn't allow it.

Acknowledgments Of
Appreciation

D URING THE TEN year period that I attended writing conferences I met several people who helped and encouraged a very late bloomer writer. Not only did their constructive criticism help me improve but their encouragement always came at a point when I wanted to give up. Special thanks to Kate Carroll DeGutes, Jamie Marshall, Ken Olsen, Gigi Rosenberg, and Renee D'Oust. Also in that same time frame I studied with two women who would frame my thoughts and discipline about writing: Dorothy Allison and Abigail Thomas. Not only are both women exceptional teachers of the craft but accomplished writers. Their mentoring and generous spirit have made everything possible.

Every writer needs trusted readers. Along the way I have had the best team ever: Joy Seidler, Carrie Applegate, Jane Poucel, Clacie England, Georgia Edwards, Merrill Moss, Rondi Egenes, Daran Davidson, Brian Adams, Scott LeMarr, Jamie McClellan, Jim Keeley, Alan Havir, Lee Ambrose, Richard Wilson, Robin Berry, and last to my sister, Sally Wakeland, who came late to the party but brought balloons.

Of course no manuscript is complete without editing. Finding Anne Horowitz was pure luck for me and the best of the best. Not only is she brilliant above and beyond but her patience and guidance made the editing process fun and educational. She refused to "just fix it" but rather always took the long way home to explain why something wasn't working and would continue ad nauseam until I got it right. Thank you, Anne, thank you. I hope to have many more for us to tackle together.

Tim and Lynda came into my life at its lowest point. Their love and care buoyed me up when I most needed it and their confidence gave me the courage to dream big. It has taken decades to be brave enough to tell Lynda's story, as she asked me to do so long ago. Special thanks to Tim for filling in the blanks and helping. I know that my many questions only unearthed painful memories for him.

Nothing would have happened if my husband, Sheldon, hadn't encouraged me to give up my day job and write full time. "You'll never get to second with your foot on first," he said. From day one he has been my biggest supporter and can always be entrusted to think of the perfect word when it escapes me. Maybe someday I will write the book he wants that would start, "On a dark and stormy night..."

Made in the USA
Las Vegas, NV
16 July 2023

74818253R00109